Enjoy!
Make-Ahead Dinner Party Menus

Enjoy!
Make-Ahead Dinner Party Menus

Nina Graybill and Maxine Rapoport

Farragut Publishing Company
Washington, D.C.
1989

PRINTED IN THE UNITED STATES OF AMERICA

Book design by Kevin Osborn

Cover illustration by Judy Barczak

Library of Congress Cataloging-in-Publication Data
Graybill, Nina.
    Enjoy! : make-ahead dinner party menus.

    1. Dinners. 2. Make-ahead cookery. 3. Menus. 4. Entertaining. I. Rapoport, Maxine. II. Title. III. Title: Make-ahead dinner party menus.
TX737.G68 1989 642'.4 88-11301
ISBN 0-918535-04-2

Second printing 1990

For Barry, as usual
N.G.

To my mother, a cook and teacher par excellence
M.R.

Introduction

*D*inner parties are one of the nicest ways to entertain—an evening of appetizing food and stimulating companionship. Yet for the host or hostess, faced with planning, preparing and serving a special meal, a dinner party can seem anything but fun.

On the appointed evening, you find yourself harried and distracted, either in the kitchen or physically among your guests but with your mind on the many things left to do.

In this book we offer a new way of planning and preparing a dinner party, one that removes the worry and rush. Our book helps you select a three-course menu perfectly suited to the occasion and to your guests. Our recipes allow you to prepare everything ahead of time, so you spend the evening enjoying your guests instead of laboring in the kitchen.

It works this way: Select your make-ahead menu from among the 36 first courses or appetizers, the 36 main courses, the 36 side dishes and the 36 desserts. As you can see, the combinations are virtually endless and almost all go together. Your choices can be based on the reason for your party (a holiday with traditional foods, for example), on your guests' likes, dislikes or special dietary needs, on the ingredients on hand, on the season, or even on your own mood.

With many of our recipes, we've suggested other courses that are especially complementary. And we've provided some sample menus to get you started. But all of these are only suggestions. Our goal is to have you select a menu that is uniquely yours.

Next, as your schedule permits, shop for and prepare the dishes you've selected. Once your guests arrive, all you will have to do is slip a pot into the oven, take a dish from the refrigerator, light the candles and call everyone to the table. We estimate that you should have to spend no more than a total of 10 minutes in the kitchen after your party begins.

That's what "make-ahead" is all about. The chopping, the sautéeing, the mixing will be over. As will arranging the table, setting up the bar, freezing the ice cubes.

To be sure you don't overlook a step before or during your party, write out a list of *everything*. Tape it to the refrigerator. Cross out what you've done as you go along. Don't forget such things as taking from the cupboard and cleaning all the serving bowls and utensils you'll be using, opening the wine, unwrapping the butter. If you have matches at hand for the candles, there'll be no last-minute scramble. In short, do everything you can in advance, no matter how small, and keep a list of what's left to do. You'll be amazed at how smoothly the evening will go.

The make-ahead recipes in this book don't call for expensive or exotic ingredients, just good food. So splurge on extra-virgin olive oil, wine vinegar, the best fresh bread you can buy, the finest fruits and vegetables—those extra touches that create memorable evenings.

All recipes in our book serve six generously, and most may be halved or made in multiples. For smaller groups, you may want to add courses—such as a salad after the main course. For larger cocktail parties, select from among the appetizers and first courses. For buffets, pick two or three main courses as different in taste, texture and ingredients as possible; you may also want to consider dishes that can be eaten using only a fork. Cost is always a factor when feeding a crowd; chicken, sausage and pasta dishes are relatively inexpensive and liked by almost everyone.

Unless otherwise specified, herbs are the whole (not ground) dried variety.

Our cookbook is designed to make entertaining not just easy, but also a pleasure. Because you will have done almost all of the work beforehand, you will be free to have a good time at your own party. And because *you* will have selected the menu, it will be just right for the evening.

Enjoy!

Nina Graybill and Maxine Rapoport

Contents

Introduction 6

Menu Suggestions 15
20 suggested menus to get you started, plus ideas to help you create menus that are uniquely yours

Appetizers 21
Marinated Green Bean and Zucchini Salad 24
Cherry Tomatoes With Parsley Pesto 25
Marinated Asparagus With Deviled Eggs 26
Chick Pea Salad 27
Roasted Peppers With Anchovies 28
Ciambotto 29
Gertie's Eggplant Salad 30
Eggplant Parmesan 31
Zena's Pickled Mushrooms 32
Layered Vegetable Pâté 33
Bean and Basil Salad 34
Black Bean Tostados 35
White Bean Purée 36
Hummous (Chick Pea Spread) 37
Tapas 38
Crostini 39
Casseri Toast 40
Tortellini With Sesame Dressing 41
Cheese and Pepper Crackers 42
Corn and Cheese Tart 43
Bourekas 44
Ceviche 45
Salmon Mousse With Mustard Mayonnaise 46
Bon Bon Chicken 47
Chicken Liver Pâté Devine 48

Baby Burritos 49
Frosted Consommé 50
Cold Curried Tomato "Soup" 51
Curried Cucumber Soup 52
Cold Cucumber and Yogurt Soup 53
Zucchini and Basil Soup 54
Cream of Asparagus or Broccoli Soup 55
Cheddar Cheese and Vegetable Soup 56
Winter Squash and Apple Soup 57
Cream of Carrot and Fresh Dill Soup 58
Mystery Zucchini Soup 59

Main Courses... 61
Roast Chicken With Garlic and Lemon 64
Tarragon Chicken Breasts With Asparagus 65
Smothered Chicken With Garlic Linda 66
Chicken in Vinegar Sauce 67
Chicken and Cabbage 68
Chicken Breasts Bloch 69
Chicken Lasagne 70
Down-Under Golden Nugget Chicken 72
Hearty Chicken Soup 73
Chicken and Smoked Sausage With Rice 74
Turkey Breast Tonnato 75
Tarragon Chicken Salad With Fruit and Nuts 76
Jambalaya 77
Italian Sausage, Shrimp and Rice Casserole 78
Sausage and Cous Cous 79
Baked Sausages and Vegetables 80
White Bean Casserole 81
Sausage and Peppers 82
Spinach Lasagne 83

Seaside Fettucine 84
Crumb-Topped Baked Fish Fillets 85
Ossobuco (Braised Veal Shanks) 86
Pasta and Veal Victoria 87
Veal Stew With Tiny Peas and Mushrooms 88
Fruited Lamb Curry 89
Lamb Shanks With Orzo 90
Moroccan Lamb Stew 91
Company Lamb Loaf With Yogurt Dill Sauce 92
Ground Beef Vegetable Garden Soup 93
Stuffed Beef Roll, Hot or Cold 94
Baked Spiced Corned Beef 95
Stifado (Greek Beef Stew) 96
Oriental Beef Stew 97
Linguine and Meat Sauce Norwood 98
Pork Carbonnade 99
Roast Pork With Game Sauce 100

Side Dishes 103
Persian Rice 106
Indian Rice 107
Rice Pilaf Deluxe 108
Baked Brown Rice With Parsley 109
Bulgur Wheat and Chick Pea Pilaf 110
Barley and Mushroom Casserole 111
French Potato Salad 112
Oven Parsley-Garlic Potatoes 113
Potato and Fruit Gratin 114
Roast Potato Wedges With Herbs 115
Potatoes With Pizazz 116
Family Favorite Potatoes 117

Noodle Casserole 118
Grits and Cheese Bake 119
Corn Pudding 120
Zucchini and Walnut Sauté 121
Winter Squash With Fruit 122
Butternut Squash and Carrot Mock Soufflé 123
Sue's Spinach Casserole 124
Mushrooms Au Gratin 125
Creamed Bermuda Onions 126
Baked Sweet Carrots 127
Baked Carrots Delicious 128
Carrot and Apple Casserole 129
Apple and Onion Casserole 130
Ratatouille 131
Vegetables Vinaigrette: A Compendium 132
Marinated Mixed Vegetables 134
Italian Toast 135

Desserts 137
Fresh Fruit Compendium 140
    Poached Pears With Raspberry Vinegar 141
    Peachy Mustard Pears 142
    Fresh Fruit Compote 143
    Strawberries and Mozzarella 144
    Berries in Berry Sauce 145
    Peaches in Spiced Chardonnay 146
    Gingered Melon 147
Figs Poached in Red Wine 148
Custard Sauce 149
Baked Fruit Compote 150
Peach or Apple and Blueberry Crisp 151
Butter Crust Apple Kuchen 152

Apple Crisp 153
Nellie's Berry Cobbler 154
Cold Orange Soufflé 155
Quick Berry Mousse With Peach Sauce 156
Low-Calorie Lemon Mousse 157
Frozen Lemon Crunch Torte With Raspberry Sauce 158
Lemon-Chocolate Charlotte 159
Layered Mocha Ice Cream Pie 160
Crème Caramel With Fresh Fruit 161
Lemony Bread Pudding 162
Chocolate Chocolate Cake 163
Devil's Food Cake Marie Larkin Connors 164
Faux Pots De Crème 165
Lime Tart 166
Peach Pie 167
Cracker Crust Pecan Pie With Mocha Cream 168
Pineapple-Coconut-Lemon Pie 169
Heavenly Hazelnut Cheesecake 170
Lucille's Shortbread 171
Dreamy Short Cookies 172
Oatmeal Lace Cookies 173
Cream Cheese And Apple Torte 174
Homey Applesauce Cake 175
Pound Cake With Lemon Glaze 176

Index 177

Menu Suggestions

Menu Suggestions

To help you get started, we've provided a number of suggested menus. When planning your own dinner, look at ingredients, textures, even colors and temperatures for the various courses and dishes. Balance light with heavy, hot with cold, spicy with mild, creamy with clear, savory with sweet. Let your menu reflect one nationality—or one region of the world. For fun, plan theme menus: red, white and blue for the Fourth of July; pastels for a spring weekend. Be kind to yourself: If one dish is time-consuming to prepare, choose quick and easy recipes for the other courses.

You'll probably want to include freshly baked bread and wine with most of your menus. We suggest, though, that you don't add much more than that: strive for a few dishes in starring roles and resist the temptation to throw in lots of bits and pieces just to make sure you'll have "enough." All our recipes serve 6 generously, and most will stretch to serve 8.

Menu #1
Marinated Green Bean and Zucchini Salad
Moroccan Lamb Stew
Indian Rice
Frozen Lemon Crunch Torte with Raspberry Sauce

Menu #2
Roasted Peppers with Anchovies
Roast Chicken with Garlic and Lemon
Corn Pudding
Apple Crisp

Menu #3
Cheese and Pepper Crackers
Jambalaya
Vegetables Vinaigrette #3
Winter Citrus Fruit Medley

_____

_____

_____

Menu #4
Crostini
Tarragon Chicken Salad with Fruit and Nuts
Baked Sweet Carrots
Faux Pots de Crème

Menu #5
Tapas
Tarragon Chicken Breasts with Asparagus
Strawberries and Mozzarella

Menu #6
Corn and Cheese Tart
Chicken in Vinegar Sauce
Vegetables Vinaigrette #1
Cold Orange Souffle

Menu #7
Cream of Carrot and Fresh Dill Soup
Chicken and Cabbage
Vegetables Vinaigrette #2
Lemony Bread Pudding with Custard Sauce

Menu #8
Cured olives, string cheese and pistachios
Sausage and Cous Cous
Figs Poached in Red Wine

Menu #9
Ceviche
Baked Sausages and Vegetables
Italian Toast
Poached Pears with Raspberry Vinegar

Menu #10
Bourekas
Stifado
Chick Pea Salad
Low Calorie Lemon Mousse

Menu #11
Winter Squash and Apple Soup
Pork Carbonnade
Bulgur Wheat with Chick Pea Pilaf
Fresh Fruit Compote

Menu #12
Marinated Asparagus with Deviled Eggs
Spinach Lasagne
Italian Toast
Peach Pie

Menu #13
Cold Curried Tomato "Soup"
Roast Pork with Game Sauce
French Potato Salad
Peach or Apple and Blueberry Crisp

Menu #14
Ciambotto with Pita Wedges
Pasta and Veal Victoria
Marinated Mixed Vegetables
Butter Crust Apple Kuchen

Menu #15
Cheddar Cheese and Vegetable Soup
Stuffed Beef Roll
Roast Potato Wedges with Herbs
Peachy Mustard Pears with Oatmeal Lace Cookies

Menu #16
Chick Pea Salad
Ossobuco
Winter Squash with Fruit
Quick Berry Mousse with Peach Sauce

Menu #17
Zena's Pickled Mushrooms and Gertie's Eggplant Salad
Company Lamb Loaf with Dill Sauce
Persian Rice
Pineapple-Coconut-Lemon Pie

Menu #18
Chicken Liver Pate Devine
Oriental Beef Stew
Baked Brown Rice with Parsley
Lime Tart

Menu #19
Baby Burritos
Hearty Chicken Soup
Basket of assorted, crunchy breads
Homey Applesauce Cake

Menu #20
Frosted Consommé
Crumb-Topped Baked Fish Fillets
Potato and Fruit Gratin
Cracker Crust Pecan Pie with Mocha Cream

Appetizers and First Courses

Appetizers and First Courses

---

*T*he only thing more appealing than a colorful first course awaiting you at a graciously set table is a tray full of tasty and interesting appetizers. Or vice versa. We have been known to consider what comes first the best part of the meal. In any case, whichever you serve, keep this in mind: Appetizers and first courses should whet the appetite, not kill it. Err on the side of too-small portions; leftovers make a fine lunch the next day. If you're serving a first course at the table, *try* to limit cocktail nibbles to olives—or nothing at all!

Marinated Green Bean and Zucchini Salad

Fresh crunchy vegetables in a piquant sauce are a wonderful start for almost any main course. The vegetables and sauce can be prepared a day or two before entertaining. Store the sauce separately so it doesn't turn the beans and zucchini "army green." Serve with thinly sliced French bread or wafers of your choice.

3/4 pound green beans, the thinner the better

2 medium zucchini

1/2 medium red onion, thinly sliced or 4 green onions, sliced

2 tablespoons capers, drained

1/3 cup olive oil

3 tablespoons tarragon or other herb vinegar

1 teaspoon basil, crushed or preferably 1 tablespoon fresh basil, chopped

2 garlic cloves, crushed

1/2 teaspoon dry mustard

1/2 teaspoon ground cumin

1 teaspoon salt

Boston or bibb lettuce for salad plates

Wash and trim beans, cut in halves or thirds. Bring small amount of water to boil in medium sauce pan. Add beans, cook 4 minutes. Drain, run under cold water to stop cooking. Drain and refrigerate, covered, for up to two days.

Scrub zucchini skin, trim ends and slice thinly. If very large, slice lengthwise first. Wrap tightly in plastic wrap or seal in a plastic bag and refrigerate up to two days.

Whisk remaining ingredients, except lettuce, in a small bowl, then cover and refrigerate.

Up to two hours before entertaining, place beans and zucchini in an appropriate bowl. Whisk salad dressing and pour over vegetables; mix gently.

Before guests arrive, line salad plates with lettuce. Just before serving time, gently stir salad and place on top of lettuce. Place thinly sliced bread on plate or pass from a basket at the table.

Serves 6.

Cherry Tomatoes
With Parsley Pesto

This is a cheerful addition to the dinner table and will go well with any entree that doesn't have tomatoes as a main ingredient.

24 medium to large cherry tomatoes, the
    brighter red the better
Curly endive or watercress for garnish

Parsley Pesto
2 cups parsley, coarse stems removed
1/2 cup walnut pieces
1/4 cup freshly grated Parmesan cheese
3 cloves garlic
1/2 teaspoon freshly ground pepper
1/2 cup olive oil

Wash tomatoes and remove small slice off the top of each. With a small spoon or tip of small knife remove seeds and any remaining pulp.

Spread a paper towel on a flat plate and place tomatoes upside down on it. Cover with plastic wrap and refrigerate up to two days.

To make pesto: In a food processor or blender process the parsley, nuts, cheese, garlic, salt and pepper. Slowly add the oil while machine is running. Taste for seasonings. Refrigerate. This can be made a week before using.

A few hours before serving, fill tomato shells with pesto. Return to plate and refrigerate until about an hour before guests arrive.

Place four tomatoes on each salad plate, garnish with endive or watercress and place plates on dining table. This salad should be served at room temperature.

Serves 6.

Marinated Asparagus With Deviled Eggs

A large platter of marinated white asparagus and deviled eggs, accompanied by great French bread and plenty of crisp white wine, once began a memorable meal in France. Perhaps you can create a little bit of Paris by serving it yourself.

2 cans of white asparagus, well drained (thin stalks if possible)
1 tablespoon Dijon-style mustard
2 tablespoons wine vinegar
4 tablespoons best quality olive oil
Salt and freshly ground black pepper to taste
18 cured black olives
7 large eggs
3 to 4 tablespoons mayonnaise
1 to 2 tablespoons Dijon-style mustard
Salt and freshly ground black pepper to taste

Make marinade for asparagus by whisking together mustard and vinegar, then slowly whisking in the olive oil until well blended. Add salt and pepper to taste. Pour over asparagus, cover and refrigerate at least one hour. Turn asparagus gently from time to time.

Place eggs in pan of cold water, bring water to a boil, reduce heat and simmer eggs for 15 minutes. Immediately run cold water over eggs; peel eggs when cool. Slice eggs in half lengthwise; remove yolks and mash in bowl with the mayonnaise, mustard and salt and pepper; taste and adjust seasonings as necessary—yolk mixture should have a fairly piquant taste. Mound or pipe yolk mixture into the best 12 white halves. Cover with plastic wrap and refrigerate until serving time.

Arrange marinated asparagus on a large white serving platter and ring with deviled eggs. Strew the black olives over the asparagus. Serve with French bread and cold white wine.

Serves 6.

Chick Pea Salad

This *makes a tasty first course all by itself—or surrounded by those ubiquitous deviled eggs. Good too as a cold vegetable side dish.*

2 cans chick peas (garbanzos), rinsed and drained
3 cloves garlic, finely minced
1 bunch scallions, sliced into rounds with some green included
1 large carrot, peeled and finely diced
1 small green pepper, seeded and finely diced
4 tablespoons wine vinegar
6 tablespoons olive oil
Salt and freshly ground pepper to taste

Combine all ingredients in a large serving bowl and blend well. Salt and pepper generously. Cover with plastic wrap and let marinate for at least one hour and preferably overnight, stirring occasionally. Check seasonings before serving and adjust as necessary.

Serves 6.

Roasted Peppers With Anchovies

Nothing looks more festive than a bowl or platter of roasted red, green and yellow sweet pepper strips, marinated in olive oil and lemon juice and garnished with anchovies. Serve chilled or at room temperature, or as part of a cold vegetable platter.

7 large sweet peppers, a mixture of green, red and yellow if possible
4 tablespoons best quality olive oil
Juice of one large lemon
Salt and freshly ground black pepper to taste
1 can flat anchovy filets, drained

Wash and dry peppers and place on broiler pan. Broil in preheated oven until skin is charred; turn peppers so all sides are roasted. Place charred peppers in a brown paper bag and close bag tightly. (Set bag in sink or on a plate in case of leakage.) When peppers are cool, wash off the charred skin under cold running water. Split peppers and discard seeds and stems. Slice peppers into long strips. Place in a serving bowl and gently blend with the olive oil, lemon juice and salt and pepper. Cover with plastic wrap and refrigerate overnight. Before serving, lay anchovy strips across top. Toss at table and serve on salad plates with lots of good bread.

Serves 6.

Ciambotto

This tangy eggplant appetizer is good with warm pita bread triangles or crisp rye crackers at cocktail time, but it is just as nice as a first course served on lettuce on a salad plate.

1/4 cup olive oil
1/8 teaspoon cayenne pepper
2 teaspoons basil
3 cloves garlic, minced
6-ounce can tomato paste
1 large onion, diced
1 large green pepper, diced
2 tablespoons red wine vinegar
1-1/2 teaspoons salt
1 large eggplant, diced into 1/2-inch cubes
1/2 cup chopped parsley
2 tablespoons capers, drained

Dice eggplant, toss with salt and let drain in a colander while preparing remaining ingredients.

Heat oil in a large skillet, add cayenne and basil and heat until aromatic, about 2 minutes.

Pat eggplant dry with paper towels and add to skillet along with tomato paste, onion, green pepper, garlic and red wine vinegar. Cover and simmer about 30 minutes. Cook somewhat longer if you want it more spreadable. Cool to room temperature, add parsley and capers and refrigerate.

This will keep well for many days and can be frozen.

Serves 6.

Gertie's Eggplant Salad

A refreshing cold eggplant dish that can be served casually on small pumpernickel "party" rounds or as a first course mounded on lettuce.

1 large, unblemished eggplant, about 1-1/2 pounds
1 medium red onion, cut in a small dice
1 large green pepper, cut in a small dice
4 tablespoons extra-virgin olive oil
Salt and freshly ground black pepper

Prick eggplant with fork and place on cookie sheet; bake in 375-degree oven until a fork penetrates the flesh easily, about 45 minutes. Let cool and scrape flesh into bowl.

Blend all ingredients, adding salt and pepper to taste. Cover and refrigerate until using.

Serves 6.

Eggplant Parmesan

This first course is a fine way to start a meal with Italian overtones: Roast Chicken with Garlic and Lemon, Italian bread, a simple green vegetable or salad, fruit and Italian macaroons—and great espresso.

2 long, unblemished eggplants, about 1-1/2 pounds total
Flour for dredging
Salt and freshly ground black pepper to taste
1/2 cup olive oil
3/4 pound whole milk mozzarella, grated
1/2 cup freshly grated Parmesan cheese

Sauce
1/4 cup olive oil
4 cloves garlic, peeled and lightly smashed
3 dried hot red peppers
28-ounce can Italian plum tomatoes
1/4 cup minced parsley

To make sauce, sauté garlic and dried peppers in the olive oil until peppers are dark brown and garlic is golden. Discard peppers and garlic. Add the tomatoes, chopping them into smaller pieces. Simmer uncovered about 20 minutes until slightly thickened. Stir occasionally. Add parsley.

While sauce is cooking, slice eggplants into 3/4-inch rounds, dredge in flour seasoned with salt and pepper. Sauté in olive oil over medium heat until nicely browned, turning once. Drain on paper towels if desired.

Coat the bottom of a shallow baking dish with some of the sauce, add the eggplant rounds in a single layer, sprinkle the mozzarella over the eggplant, then cover with more sauce. Sprinkle the parmesan cheese over all. Cover with foil and refrigerate for up to 3 days.

About 45 minutes before serving, bake covered in a 375-degree oven for 30 minutes, then remove foil for last 15 minutes of baking time. Serve one or two rounds, with some of the sauce, per person.

Serves 6.

Zena's Pickled Mushrooms

This very low-calorie appetizer can stand alone or as part of an hors d'oeuvres selection, to be served on a large tray with drinks before dinner.

1 pound small mushrooms, cleaned and stems trimmed
2 cups water
1 teaspoon salt (optional)
1/4 cup white wine vinegar
2 tablespoons olive oil
1/2 teaspoon salt
1/4 teaspoon oregano, crushed
1/8 teaspoon pepper
1 tablespoon chopped parsley
1 clove garlic, minced

Bring water and optional salt to a boil, add mushrooms and simmer for 5 minutes. Drain well and add to the remaining ingredients which have been stirred together. Refrigerate at least overnight or several days. Serve slightly chilled.

Serves 6.

Layered Vegetable Pâté

This variation of an old favorite, gazpacho, can be your first course as well as a salad. You might serve this with the Roast Pork with Game Sauce.

3 cups canned plum tomatoes with their juice
1 medium green pepper, cut into eighths
1 cucumber, peeled, seeded and cut into large pieces
1 medium white onion, cut into quarters
2 tablespoons olive oil
3 tablespoons tomato paste
3 tablespoons red wine vinegar
1 tablespoon salt
2 teaspoons ground cumin
1/2 teaspoon celery seed
1/4 teaspoon cayenne pepper
3 packages, or 3 tablespoons, unflavored gelatin
1/2 cup dry white wine
1 ripe but not soft avocado, peeled, pitted and cubed
1 medium green or yellow sweet pepper, minced
Shredded lettuce for garnish

Purée in a food processor (or purée in two batches in a blender) the plum tomatoes, green pepper, cucumber, onion, olive oil, vinegar, salt, cumin, celery seed and cayenne. Transfer to a large bowl.

In a small bowl soften the gelatin with the wine by placing it into a larger bowl filled with hot water. Stir until dissolved.

Combine the vegetable purée with the softened gelatin. Add the cubed avocado and minced green pepper. Oil a 9 x 5 inch loaf pan and pour in the mixture. Chill up to several days before serving.

Run a small knife around the pan and dip the pan into a larger pan of hot water for a couple of seconds. Invert onto a platter. Slice pâté about an inch thick and place on individual salad plates garnished with shredded lettuce. Place a dollop of good mayonnaise alongside the pâté.

Serves 6.

Bean and Basil Salad

This colorful first course takes on a Latin air when served with crisp tortilla chips. You might want to pursue this theme with the Roast Pork with Game Sauce and your favorite rice salad.

16-ounce can white beans, rinsed and drained
16-ounce can red beans, rinsed and drained
1/2 cup olive oil
1/4 cup red wine vinegar
1 tablespoon lemon juice
2 tablespoons basil, crushed, or 4 tablespoons finely chopped fresh basil
1/2 teaspoon sugar
1/2 to 1 teaspoon salt
1/2 teaspoon red pepper flakes
4 cloves garlic, minced
Shredded iceberg lettuce
Tortilla chips or thinly sliced French bread

Combine all but last two ingredients and refrigerate at least 24 hours. Bring to room temperature and taste for seasonings; adjust if necessary. Divide shredded lettuce on salad plates, spoon beans on top. Pass tortilla chips separately.

Serves 6.

Black Bean Tostados

A single tostado makes a colorful and tasty first course. Two or three could equal lunch or dinner. Commercially prepared ingredients make this dish a snap.

6 packaged tostados (flat taco shells)
1 can black beans
6 ounces Monterey Jack cheese, shredded
6 tablespoons prepared Mexican salsa, preferably made with cilantro
6 tablespoons sour cream
6 tablespoons frozen avocado dip, thawed, or one small ripe avocado, cut in a small dice and sprinkled with lemon juice
1 medium tomato, cut in a small dice

Place the tostados on a cookie sheet. Drain the beans well and divide among the tostados. Sprinkle the shredded cheese over all. Cover with plastic wrap and refrigerate.

About 10 minutes before serving, bake tostados in a preheated 375-degree oven until cheese is bubbling.

Put one tablespoon each of salsa, sour cream, avocado dip or fresh avocado, and diced tomato on top of each tostado. Serve on individual salad plates.

Serves 6.

White Bean Purée

A food processor or blender makes short work of this hearty purée, which can be used as a dip for crackers, chips or vegetables or as part of a cold vegetable platter served as a first course or side dish. Deviled eggs are especially tasty with it.

2 cups small white beans, canned or home cooked, drained (reserve liquid)
3 tablespoons olive oil
2 small cloves garlic, minced
1 tablespoon lemon juice
1/4 teaspoon leaf thyme
1/4 teaspoon basil
1/4 teaspoon coriander
Salt and freshly ground black pepper to taste
1/4 cup minced fresh parsley
Several dashes hot pepper sauce, optional

Place all ingredients in the container of a food processor or blender and blend until smooth. Add reserved bean liquid a little at a time if necessary. Mixture should be thick. Taste and adjust seasonings, keeping in mind that flavors will intensify over time. Cover with plastic wrap and refrigerate at least 24 hours.

Serves 6.

Hummous (Chick Pea Spread)

Another purée of beans—this one, the Middle Eastern hummous, calls for tahini, or sesame seed paste, available in most large supermarkets or specialty markets. Serve with warm pita triangles or vegetable sticks.

2 cans chick peas, drained but with liquid reserved
1/2 cup tahini
1 tablespoon olive oil, plus 2 more for garnish
Juice of one lemon
3 cloves of garlic, minced
1/2 teaspoon cumin
1/8 teaspoon cayenne pepper
Salt to taste
1/2 cup minced parsley
18 cured black olives

In a blender or food processor, blend together all ingredients except the parsley, olives and 2 tablespoons olive oil. If necessary, add bean liquid a little at a time, until the mixture reaches the right consistency for dipping without dripping. Taste for seasonings and adjust as necessary, keeping in mind flavors will intensify over time.

Spread into a round shallow bowl. Spoon two tablespoons olive oil over top. Spread the minced parsley around the edge of the hummous and make a circle of parsley in the center. Place the olives in a ring between the two parsley circles. Cover with plastic wrap and refrigerate overnight. Serve with pita bread or raw vegetables.

Serves 6 or more.

Tapas

If you're looking for something simple but different, consider starting the meal with Spanish-type appetizers and a glass of dry sherry. Choose four to six items from the list below, arrange in small bowls or platters on a tray, provide your guests with plates and forks and let them select their favorites. For you, it will be mostly a matter of wielding a can opener.

4 ounces each best quality black and green cured olives
1 pound small spiced shrimp, cooked, peeled and chilled (may be purchased already prepared)
1 can smoked oysters, drained
1 can skinless and boneless sardines, drained
1 can anchovies, drained
1 cup shelled and salted nuts, such as almonds, filberts or pecans
1 jar hot pickled okra
Pepperoni slices
12 slices prosciutto wrapped around 12 melon wedges
Deviled eggs (see recipe in this section)
9-ounce jar pickled vegetables (Italian giardinera), drained
Syrian string cheese
8 ounces bleu cheese, cut into bite-size cubes or wedges
1 jar marinated artichoke hearts, drained

Serves 6.

Crostini

Sophisticated "cheese toast" to munch with drinks, or to serve as a first course at the table, using knives and forks.

12 1/2-inch slices best quality Italian bread
12 scant teaspoons extra-virgin olive oil
12 1/4-inch slices whole milk mozzarella cheese to fit bread
1 can of flat anchovies, drained and sliced lengthwise so you have 24 slivers
12 pats of butter

Spread a teaspoon of oil on each bread slice. Place a slice of cheese on the bread, place two pieces of anchovy on the cheese in an "x" shape, and top all with a pat of butter. Place bread on a cookie sheet. Cover with plastic wrap, refrigerate overnight.

Ten minutes before serving, unwrap and place in a preheated 375-degree oven. Bake until cheese is bubbly and bottom of bread is lightly browned.

Serves 6.

Casseri Toast

Casseri is a salty Greek cheese. Be sure you buy an imported brand—domestic Casseri is not nearly so good.

12 ounces imported Casseri cheese
12 1/2-inch slices good French baguette (about 2 inches in diameter)
4 tablespoons olive oil
1 teaspoon dried leaf oregano

Slice the French bread rounds in half again crosswise, for a total of 24 pieces. Place on cookie sheet in 300-degree oven and bake about 10 to 15 minutes until bread has crisped. Remove.

Grate Casseri and put in a heavy skillet; add olive oil and oregano. Melt over very low heat, stirring occasionally.

Dip one side of the bread in the cheese mixture, making sure each piece has oil and cheese on it. Replace bread on cookie sheet, cover with plastic wrap and refrigerate.

To serve, remove plastic wrap and heat bread in a 350-degree oven about 10 minutes or until hot. Place in a basket lined with a cloth napkin and offer your guests cocktail napkins along with the toast.

Serves 6.

Tortellini With Sesame Dressing

This unusual first course requires no time-consuming preparation and can be assembled the day before. Most supermarkets carry fresh but packaged pasta—or try the local Italian grocer. Roast chicken or leg of lamb with oregano would be a nice entree.

1 pound cheese-filled tortellini
2 sweet red peppers, thinly sliced
1/2 cup cured Italian black olives
2 tablespoons salad oil
1/2 cup chopped green onions

Dressing
2 cloves garlic, minced
2 teaspoons sesame seeds
1/2 cup olive oil
3 tablespoons white wine vinegar
1 teaspoon salt
Freshly ground pepper, about 1/4 teaspoon or to taste

Cook the pasta in boiling salted water, 5 to 10 minutes for fresh, 10 to 15 minutes for frozen. Test before draining. Drain and rinse with cold water. Toss with 2 tablespoons salad oil. Cover tightly and refrigerate.

Slice peppers, chop green onions, wrap separately and refrigerate.

In a small skillet, heat the olive oil over medium heat, add the garlic and sesame seeds and remove from heat when garlic and seeds start to brown. When the oil mixture cools, whisk in the vinegar, salt and pepper. Refrigerate.

Two hours before serving, remove dressing and whisk thoroughly. Combine tortellini, peppers, green onions, olives and dressing.

At least one hour before guests arrive, arrange 4 tortellini and some of the vegetables on each salad plate. Serve at room temperature.

Serves 6.

Cheese and Pepper Crackers

Tasty little cocktail treats. A good way to use up leftover bits of cheese, or try all one kind, such as sharp Cheddar or Brie.

1 stick butter, at room temperature
4 ounces (approximately) grated hard cheese, or soft cheese at room temperature
1 cup flour (approximately)
1/8 teaspoon cayenne pepper (1 teaspoon dried dillweed may be substituted)
Dash of salt

Blend together the softened butter, the cheese and the seasonings. Add flour gradually and mix thoroughly until you have a stiff batter. Divide mixture in half, roll each half into a log about 1 inch in diameter. Roll logs in plastic wrap and chill thoroughly, at least overnight.

Preheat oven to 375 degrees. Slice cheese logs into rounds about 1/4 inch thick. Bake on a cookie sheet 8 to 10 minutes. Cool, then store in a tightly covered container.

Makes about 60 crackers.

Corn and Cheese Tart

*N*one dare call it quiche these days. This is a simple and tasty pie that avoids the over-rich excesses of some quiches. It is best served warm. Variations on this tart include frozen chopped spinach, thawed and squeezed dry and seasoned with salt, pepper and a dash of nutmeg, or frozen chopped broccoli, lightly cooked, drained well and seasoned with salt, pepper and butter.

One ready-made, deep-dish frozen pie shell, thawed
1 box frozen corn kernels
1 tablespoon butter
4 ounces mild white cheese, such as Monterey Jack, grated
3 large eggs
3/4 cup half and half or whole milk
Salt and freshly ground pepper to taste

Press thawed pie crust into an 8-inch tart pan; crimp edges. Prick all over with fork and prebake in 425-degree oven for about 10 minutes, just until shell begins to color. Place on cookie sheet and set aside.

Cook frozen corn in a small amount of boiling water for about 3 minutes. Drain; season well with the butter, salt and pepper.

Whisk eggs until lightly blended; add milk and grated cheese. Add corn by tablespoons so it doesn't cook eggs. Pour egg mixture into tart shell. Place cookie sheet with tart pan in preheated 350-degree oven. Bake tart about 30-35 minutes or until knife inserted near center comes out clean. Let cool, cover and refrigerate.

Twenty minutes before serving, place in 350-degree oven to heat through. May also be served at room temperature.

Serves 6.

Bourekas (Cheese Triangles)

These trim triangles of feta cheese in phyllo leaves are a Middle Eastern treat. They freeze well, so make a double batch and you'll have some on hand for drop-in guests. Serve warm with cocktails or as a first course.

1/2 pound frozen phyllo dough
1 stick (or more) melted butter
2 large eggs
1 cup small curd cottage cheese, drained if there is a lot of liquid
1/2 pound feta cheese, drained and crumbled
1/8 to 1/4 teaspoon cayenne pepper

Let the phyllo dough come to room temperature while still wrapped in its packaging or in plastic wrap. (Do not allow phyllo to dry out or it will crumble instead of fold.)

In a medium-sized bowl, beat eggs well. Add the two cheeses and blend. Add the cayenne pepper to taste, a little at a time; taste mixture between additions—it should be zippy.

Cut the phyllo sheets into strips about 3 inches wide. Work quickly with one stack of phyllo strips at a time; keep the others under a damp towel.

Brush one strip of phyllo with melted butter and place a teaspoon of the cheese mixture in one end. Fold the ends over into a triangle, as you would fold a flag. (Don't worry about the messy ones—they'll still taste good!) Repeat until all the cheese mixture is used. (Leftover phyllo can be resealed tightly and refrozen.)

Place triangles on a cookie sheet in one layer and freeze. Transfer to foil or freezer bags and wrap well. Store in freezer.

About 20 minutes before serving, place the triangles on a cookie sheet and bake until golden in a preheated 400-degree oven.

Makes about 4 dozen bourekas.

Ceviche

Raw fish fillets "cooked" in lime juice and spiced with chili peppers and cilantro. This Latin classic is becoming more and more familiar to American palates—and with good reason: It's delicious!

1-1/2 pounds fillet of any non-oily, firm fish, such as flounder, grouper or red
    snapper
Juice of 4 limes
Salt and freshly ground black pepper to taste
4 tablespoons olive oil
2 canned serrano chili peppers, seeded and chopped fine
2 large ripe tomatoes, peeled, seeded and chopped*
1/2 teaspoon oregano
1 medium red onion, peeled and thinly sliced
2 tablespoons chopped fresh coriander (cilantro or Chinese parsley)
Capers and lime slices for garnish

Cut the fish fillets into bite-size pieces, about 1 inch square. Place in glass bowl and cover with the lime juice. Let marinate, refrigerated, for about 4 hours, turning fish from time to time.

Add the rest of the ingredients, mix gently, cover and refrigerate for up to 24 hours. *To peel tomatoes easily, drop in boiling water for 10 to 20 seconds; skin will slip off.

Divide among six glass or white salad plates; garnish with capers and thin slices of lime if desired.

Serves 6.

Salmon Mousse
With Mustard Mayonnaise

An elegant first course. Serve with Chicken Breasts Bloch, rice pilaf and for dessert, Lemon-Chocolate Charlotte.

16-ounce can red salmon, drained and liquid reserved
1 envelope unflavored gelatin
3 tablespoons salmon liquid
3 tablespoons boiling water
2 tablespoons each lemon juice and vinegar
1/2 teaspoon salt
1-1/2 teaspoons sugar
1 tablespoon finely chopped onion
2 teaspoons horseradish
1 tablespoon chopped fresh dill or 1 teaspoon dried dillweed
1/4 cup finely sliced celery
1 cup good mayonnaise

Mustard Mayonnaise
1 cup good mayonnaise, preferably homemade
4 tablespoons Dijon mustard
1 tablespoon lemon juice
1/2 teaspoon sugar
1 tablespoon chopped fresh dill or 1 teaspoon dried dillweed

Mix Mustard Mayonnaise ingredients and refrigerate until needed.

Soften gelatin in salmon liquid in a medium-sized bowl. Add boiling water and stir until dissolved. Mix in the lemon juice and vinegar, salt, sugar, onion and horseradish. Cool until slightly thickened. Stir in flaked salmon, mayonnaise and fresh or dried dill. Turn into a well-oiled 5 x 9 inch loaf pan and cover with plastic wrap.

Chill overnight or for several days. Remove from mold, slice 1/2 inch thick and place on individual salad plates. Garnish with greens, dill sprigs and a dollop of Mustard Mayonnaise. Pass additional sauce.

Serves 6.

Bon Bon Chicken

Chilled chicken breast slivers in a spicy sesame sauce, served on a bed of lettuce, is an unusual way to begin dinner. Mix the chicken with 12 ounces cooked linguine, and you have a main course pasta salad. This is just what we did in our first cookbook, The Pasta Salad Book. *Eat with chopsticks for an authentic touch.*

1-1/2 pounds boned and skinned chicken breasts
1/2 cup sesame paste (either Chinese style or the Middle Eastern tahini)
3 tablespoons water
1 teaspoon Chinese hot oil, or to taste
5 tablespoons soy sauce
3 tablespoons white wine vinegar
1/4 cup salad oil
3 large cloves garlic, minced
Lettuce, optional

Poach the chicken breasts in seasoned simmering water until just tender, about 15 minutes. Cool and tear or cut meat into thin strips.

Blend the sesame paste with water, then add the rest of the sauce ingredients and mix well. Pour over chicken, toss to coat well, and chill at least four hours or overnight.

Serve on a bed of shredded lettuce on individual salad plates, if desired.

Serves 6.

Chicken Liver Pâté Devine

This is not a true pâté as it is not baked, but it is delicious. Serve this with dark bread at cocktail time or on salad plates with lettuce and cornichon garnish as a more formal first course. Pass crisp rye crackers.

1 pound chicken livers, trimmed of membrane and fat
1 teaspoon dried dillweed or 4 sprigs fresh dill, snipped
1/2 teaspoon pepper
1/2 teaspoon ground cloves
1/2 teaspoon ground ginger
1/4 teaspoon ground nutmeg
1/2 teaspoon sage, crushed, or poultry seasoning
1/4 teaspoon salt
1 heaping teaspoon Dijon mustard
4 tablespoons butter, softened
4 cloves garlic, minced
1/2 jigger brandy (optional) (1 jigger = 1-1/2 ounces)

Simmer chicken livers about 10 minutes in small amount of water. Drain thoroughly and chop in food processor or food grinder. Add remaining ingredients in order given. Mix until smooth either in food processor or with electric mixer.

Cover tightly with plastic and foil. Refrigerate up to four days or freeze.

Pack into an attractive mold or serving bowl if serving with drinks. If serving at the table as a first course, scoop out in rounded servings onto lettuce.

Serves 6.

Baby Burritos

An obvious first course with a Mexican or Latin dinner menu, but good too in a tapas assortment with drinks.

1 pound lean ground beef
1/2 cup chopped onion
1/2 cup finely chopped green pepper
1/2 teaspoon salt
1 teaspoon oregano
2 teaspoons chili powder
1/2 teaspoon ground cumin

1/2 of a 15-ounce can of refried beans
1/2 cup shredded sharp Cheddar cheese
2 tablespoons chili sauce or catsup
1 package won ton skins (usually 55 to 60 in package)
Cooking oil for frying

In a large skillet, cook ground beef, onion and green pepper until meat is brown; drain grease. Stir in salt, oregano, chili powder, cumin, beans, cheese and chili sauce or catsup; mix well.

To fill won ton skins, place one skin at a time on a plate with one point toward you. Place a teaspoon of filling in center and fold sides over filling; moisten last point with water and press to seal.

Heat about 1 inch of oil in a medium-size skillet until almost smoking, or a drop of cold water sizzles in the oil. Fry about five or six burritos at a time, turning with a slotted spoon and fork after one minute, until just golden. Remove with a slotted spoon to paper towels.

When burritos are cool, store, covered, in refrigerator for a few days; for a longer period, put in an airtight container or wrap well in foil and freeze.

Preheat oven to 350 degrees, place refrigerated or frozen burritos on a cookie sheet and bake, loosely covered with foil, for 10 minutes. Serve with salsa.

Makes 55 to 60 burritos.

Frosted Consommé

This elegant, easy first course works well with Roast Chicken With Garlic and Lemon.

3 10-1/2 ounce cans of beef consommé with gelatin
3 ounces cream cheese, softened
3 tablespoons finely chopped green onion tops
1 tablespoon chopped parsley

At least two days before serving, mix 2 cans consommé with cream cheese just until well blended, and pour into six small soup bowls, preferably clear glass. Cover with plastic wrap and refrigerate until set.

The night before serving, mix the remaining can of consommé with the chopped onion tops and parsley. Spoon an equal amount of the mixture into each bowl and again chill until set.

Serves 6.

Cold Curried Tomato "Soup"

This sensational first course should only be served in the summer when tomatoes are at their peak—but it's worth the wait through the cold winter. Great with a simple outdoor grilled entree or pasta salad.

8 medium to large ripe tomatoes, peeled
1 medium to large onion
1 teaspoon salt, or to taste
1/4 to 1/2 teaspoon freshly ground pepper
3/4 cup good mayonnaise
2 teaspoons curry powder, or to taste
1 teaspoon tarragon, crushed

Early in the day or at least 3 hours before serving, peel tomatoes with a swivel-type peeler. Chop and put into a large bowl. Grate or finely chop onion and add with salt and pepper to tomatoes. Refrigerate.

In a small bowl, mix mayonnaise with curry powder and tarragon; refrigerate.

To serve, spoon tomato mixture into small bowls, and top with a dollop of curried mayonnaise. Have your guests mix the mayonnaise into the soup.

Serves 6.

Curried Cucumber Soup

This simple and versatile cold soup could serve as a first course for your favorite grilled dinner.

3 cucumbers, peeled, quartered and seeded
2 10-3/4 ounce cans chicken broth (or homemade)
1/4 cup chopped onions
1-1/2 teaspoons curry powder
1 teaspoon dillweed or 1 tablespoon fresh dill, chopped
1 cup plain yogurt
1/2 teaspoon salt or more to taste
Fresh mint, chopped, for garnish

Put cucumbers and chicken broth in a 3-quart kettle. Add onions and seasonings. Cover and cook over moderate heat about 10 minutes, until cucumbers are soft. Set aside to cool.

Put small amounts into food processor or blender with part of yogurt. Purée until smooth. Transfer to a bowl or pitcher and repeat with remaining soup and yogurt.

Refrigerate until serving time. Taste for salt before serving and adjust to taste.

Garnish with fresh mint.

Serves 6.

Cold Cucumber and Yogurt Soup

A nother cold cucumber soup, though this one requires no cooking. A good way to begin a meal based on Greek or other Middle Eastern cuisines. Halve the amount of yogurt, and the soup becomes a side dish or salad.

3 cucumbers, peeled, cut in half lengthwise, and seeds removed
2 cloves garlic, minced fine
3 cups yogurt
2 tablespoons olive oil
1/2 teaspoon salt
1 teaspoon white vinegar
3 tablespoons snipped fresh dill
3 tablespoons minced parsley
12 mint leaves, optional, for garnish
12 very thin slices of unpeeled cucumber, optional, for garnish

Slice each cucumber half lengthwise into four strips. Cut crosswise into a small dice. Blend with rest of ingredients, except garnishes. Cover and chill overnight. After flavors have blended, taste for seasonings and adjust as necessary. Ladle into six small bowls and garnish with the mint leaves or float the cucumber slices on top.

Serves 6.

Zucchini and Basil Soup

This soup is equally good served hot or cold. It works well with a seafood pasta salad. If you serve the soup cold for a summer menu, by all means use the fresh basil.

6 cups thinly sliced scrubbed zucchini
3 cups chicken broth, fat removed
1/2 cup fresh basil leaves, or 2 tablespoons dried
2 tablespoons fresh lemon juice
1-1/2 teaspoon salt
Sour cream for garnish

Put zucchini, broth, basil and salt into a kettle. Bring to a boil, then simmer uncovered about 10 minutes. Cool.

Transfer in batches to food processor or blender and purée. Add lemon juice and refrigerate until ready to use. If serving hot, reheat slowly. Taste for seasoning, especially if serving cold.

Serves 6.

Cream of Asparagus
or Broccoli Soup

_____

_____

_____

Either of these silky soups can be served hot or cold. Low-calorie they are not, so ease your conscience by serving a light fruit dessert.

1-1/2 pounds fresh asparagus or fresh broccoli
5 cups chicken broth (canned is fine)
1 cup heavy cream
Salt and freshly ground pepper to taste
Sour cream, optional
Fresh snipped dill, optional

If you are using asparagus, snap off white part of stalk, wash, and slice each stalk into three pieces. Wash the broccoli and peel the lower stalks; break apart the flower. Place the asparagus or broccoli in the chicken broth and simmer until vegetable is soft (about 12 minutes). Transfer the vegetables and about 1 cup of the broth to the container of a blender or food processor and blend until smooth. Return puréed vegetable to rest of chicken broth and simmer another 10 minutes. Add salt and pepper to taste. Add heavy cream and simmer a few more minutes. Let cool, cover and refrigerate, at least overnight.

Taste again for seasonings and adjust if necessary. Reheat slowly until just simmering, or serve cold. Ladle into cream soup bowls, and garnish with a dollop of sour cream and fresh dill, if desired.

Serves 6.

Cheddar Cheese and Vegetable Soup

Take your pick when serving this first course: chunky or smooth, hot or cold.

3 tablespoons butter or margarine
1/2 cup chopped onion
1/2 cup chopped carrots
1/4 cup finely chopped green pepper
1/4 cup finely chopped celery
3 tablespoons flour
4 10-3/4-ounce cans chicken broth or 5 cups homemade chicken stock
1/2 pound sharp Cheddar cheese, coarsely grated
1-1/2 cups milk
1/2 teaspoon marjoram
Salt and white pepper to taste
Coriander or parsley finely chopped for garnish

In 3-quart kettle, melt butter or margarine over moderate heat. Add onion, carrot, green pepper and celery and cook until vegetables are limp and golden; off heat, blend in flour, return to heat and slowly add broth; mix until blended. Bring to a boil and cook until slightly thickened, stirring frequently. Reduce heat, add marjoram and partially cover. Simmer about 10 minutes, stirring occasionally.

Slowly add grated cheese and cook until all is melted. Add 1 cup milk, adding the remaining 1/2 cup if soup is too thick. Bring to a slight boil and remove from heat.

Taste for salt and pepper and season if necessary. If you plan to serve the soup smooth, cool before whirling in small batches in a food processor or blender. Refrigerate. If serving cold, taste for salt and pepper before serving and adjust to taste. If serving hot, either chunky or smooth, reheat very slowly, stirring occasionally.

Serves 6.

Winter Squash and Apple Soup

*Y*our guests may have a hard time identifying the ingredients, but they won't be disappointed by the flavor of this soup. For midwinter entertaining, serve the soup hot, followed by Stifado. Try it chilled with an entree of pasta salad for summer dining.

3 cups winter squash, butternut or hubbard
3 green apples, Greening or Granny Smith
3 10-3/4-ounce cans chicken broth, fat removed
1/2 cup water
3 slices bread, white or wheat, crusts removed, diced
3/4 cup chopped onion
1 teaspoon salt
Scant 1/4 teaspoon rosemary
1/2 teaspoon marjoram
Chopped parsley for garnish

Halve squash, remove seeds and peel; cut into large cubes. Peel, core and roughly chop apples. In a 4-quart kettle combine squash, apples, chicken broth, water, bread cubes, salt, pepper, rosemary and marjoram. Slowly bring to a boil, reduce heat and simmer, uncovered, about 30 minutes. Cool.

Purée in small batches in food processor or blender. Transfer each batch to a large container and refrigerate or freeze until ready to use. Thaw if frozen and reheat slowly.

If frozen and serving cold, thaw and spin in food processor or blender to blend separated ingredients.

Serves 6.

Cream of Carrot
and Fresh Dill Soup

Fresh dill is a must for this hot or cold soup. You might use this with the Baked Spiced Corned Beef.

1 pound carrots, scraped and thinly sliced
1 cup chopped onions
2 tablespoons butter or margarine
2 10-3/4 ounce cans chicken broth, fat removed
1 teaspoon salt
1/2 cup table cream
1/2 cup milk
2 tablespoons finely chopped fresh dill
1/8 to 1/4 teaspoon cayenne pepper

Heat the butter in a medium-sized kettle and cook the onions just until transparent. Add the carrots, chicken broth and salt. Bring to a boil, then simmer 15 minutes. Cool.

Pour manageable batches into a food processor or blender and purée. Transfer each batch to a large bowl. Add cream, milk, dill and cayenne and mix thoroughly.

Refrigerate until ready to use. Taste for seasoning, especially if serving cold as cold dishes require more intense seasoning. If serving hot, heat very slowly to prevent sticking.

Serves 6.

Mystery Zucchini Soup

Might be fun to have your guests guess the mystery ingredient (bacon). This is the perfect foil for Stuffed Beef Roll.

3 cups coarsely diced zucchini
2 strips bacon, halved
2 10-1/2 ounce cans beef broth
1 medium onion, chopped
2 cloves garlic, minced
1 tablespoon chopped fresh basil or 1-1/2 teaspoons dried basil
1 teaspoon salt
1/2 teaspoon pepper

Put all ingredients into medium-sized kettle, bring to a gentle boil, then reduce heat and simmer about 20 minutes. Cool before transferring in small batches to food processor or blender to purée. Taste for seasoning and adjust if necessary.

Refrigerate or freeze until ready to use. Thaw, then reheat very slowly, stirring occasionally.

Serves 6.

Main Courses

Main Courses

*M*any of these main courses are complete entrees in themselves. If you want to add a side dish, see the next section. Or serve a simple green salad as a separate course before dessert. Freshly baked bread and the wine of your choice are always welcome additions.

Roast Chicken
With Garlic and Lemon

Roast chicken need not be the bland, overdone Sunday dinner standard. Whole frying chickens, quickly browned in a hot oven, take on an entirely new image. Add a spoonful or two of a simple sauce made from the flavorful cooking juices and you'll never bake chicken any other way.

2 whole frying chickens, about 3 pounds each
Olive oil
Salt and freshly ground black pepper
8 cloves of garlic, peeled and lightly mashed
2 lemons at room temperature, quartered and seeds removed
2 teaspoons rosemary leaves
1 cup chicken broth

Place birds in shallow roasting pan. Rub all over with olive oil, then salt and pepper liberally; sprinkle 1/2 teaspoon rosemary over each chicken. In cavity of each bird, place a quartered lemon, 1/2 teaspoon of rosemary, and 3 cloves of garlic. Place remaining garlic in roasting pan. Cover with plastic wrap and refrigerate until 1-1/2 hours before serving.

Preheat oven to 400 degrees. Bake chicken, uncovered, for about 50-60 minutes. Chicken is done when it is well-browned and thigh juices run clear. Carefully drain cavities of their juices, lemon pieces and garlic into roasting pan. Place chickens on a serving platter and let rest while you make the sauce. With back of a wooden spoon, press lemons and garlic into pan; discard lemon rinds and any garlic that is not soft. Add chicken broth; raise heat and boil mixture, stirring up the browned bits in the roasting pan, until mixture reduces to a light syrup. There should be about two tablespoons of sauce per serving.

A tip if you're not handy at carving: Using poultry shears, quickly divide birds in half and in half again crosswise, so that each serving piece consists of a leg quarter or a breast quarter. Serve each guest his or her favorite type with a little sauce spooned over.

Serves 6.

Tarragon Chicken Breasts With Asparagus

This is a perfect dish to serve during asparagus season. Rice or wheat pilaf and baked cherry tomatoes seasoned with olive oil and dill make tasty side dishes.

6 chicken breast halves, boned but with skin left on
24 stalks of asparagus, washed and trimmed
1 stick butter, at room temperature
2 tablespoons tarragon, or 4 tablespoons fresh minced tarragon
Salt and freshly ground black pepper
Parsley sprigs and lemon rounds for garnish
1 recipe blender hollandaise sauce, at room temperature (see directions below)

Lightly flatten chicken breasts. Blend butter and tarragon in small bowl. Divide mixture into six portions and spread on interior of each breast. Sprinkle with salt and pepper to taste. Place four asparagus stalks in each chicken breast, fold breast over and secure with a toothpick. Spread any left-over butter on top skin of chicken. Place breasts in well-oiled baking dish, cover with plastic wrap and refrigerate until one hour before serving.

To cook chicken, place in preheated 375-degree oven and bake uncovered for about 45 minutes, until kitchen fork inserts easily and chicken is nicely browned. (Remove toothpicks or warn your guests!)

To make blender hollandaise, place three egg yolks, juice of one lemon, dash of cayenne pepper, 1 teaspoon salt in container of blender or food processor and blend briefly. Melt 1-1/2 sticks of butter until bubbly, being careful not to brown it. With blender running, slowly pour hot butter into egg mixture until well blended. Place sauce in serving container, cover with plastic wrap, and keep at room temperature until serving time. May be made up to three hours in advance.

To serve, place chicken on warm platter and garnish with the parsley and lemon. Pass the hollandaise sauce separately.

Serves 6.

Smothered Chicken
With Garlic Linda

This simple chicken casserole makes a dramatic entrance, sealed as it is with a flour rope. The seal is broken at table, the top of the casserole lifted and the heady fragrance of chicken, garlic and herbs fills the air.

1 large roasting chicken, about 6 pounds
Salt and freshly ground black pepper to taste
5 heads of garlic, separated, with papery skins discarded
3 bay leaves
1 tablespoon rosemary
1 teaspoon each thyme and marjoram
1 cup olive oil

Flour paste
3-1/2 cups of flour
Water as needed, about 2 cups

Salt and pepper chicken well. Place bird in large flame-proof casserole with cover, and tuck the wings under the body. Distribute the garlic cloves and the seasonings over and around the chicken, then drizzle the olive oil over all. Cover.

Make a firm but pliable flour paste by slowly stirring the water into the flour. Oil hands so paste won't stick to them. Form a long rope about 2 inches thick and press the rope over the opening between the casserole and the cover to form a tight seal. Refrigerate the casserole if not baking the chicken immediately.

Two hours before serving, preheat the oven to 350 degrees. Heat the casserole on top of the stove until you hear the oil sizzle, then place in oven. Cook the chicken for about 2 hours.

To serve, take the sealed casserole to the table, break the seal and remove the bird to a serving platter. Carve swiftly, and serve each portion with a spoonful or two of the oil and several cloves of garlic.

Serves 6.

Chicken in Vinegar Sauce

*O*ne *of our most-asked-for recipes, this chicken dish can be the basis of a rather formal meal when served with rice or on a bed of sautéed polenta (see discussion of polenta on page 82). Much more fun, we think, is to serve it with great French or Italian bread to be dipped in the sauce.*

6 large chicken breast halves, cut in half again crosswise
3 tablespoons olive oil
4 cloves garlic, peeled and lightly mashed
1 tablespoon rosemary leaves, lightly crushed
Salt and freshly ground black pepper to taste
1/2 cup red wine vinegar
1/2 cup dry white wine (dry vermouth is fine)
1/4 cup minced parsley (optional)

In an ovenproof skillet large enough to hold the chicken pieces in one layer, lightly brown the garlic in the olive oil; discard garlic.

Place the chicken pieces, skin side up, in the flavored oil. Sprinkle the rosemary and salt and pepper on top of the chicken. Brown both sides well over medium heat. Add wine and vinegar. (If you are not serving immediately, cool, cover and refrigerate until 45 minutes before dinner.)

Bring chicken, wine and vinegar to a boil on top of the stove, then place in 375-degree oven and bake, covered, until tender, about 25 to 30 minutes.

Remove chicken to a serving platter. Bring vinegar and wine sauce to a boil on top of the stove, stirring, until sauce thickens slightly. Pour sauce over chicken, and sprinkle with parsley if desired.

Serves 6.

Chicken and Cabbage

Cabbage for company? Of course, especially when it's cooked to a rich and mellow succulence and full of juicy morsels of chicken. You can vary this dish by using best quality sausage links or a combination of chicken and sausage.

1 large head cabbage, green or red, about 3 pounds, sliced into long quarter-
    inch-wide shreds
2 large onions, peeled and sliced thin
3 cloves garlic, minced
1/4 cup olive oil
3/4 cup dry white or red wine (depending on your choice of cabbage)
1/4 cup wine vinegar
6 chicken breast halves, bone in but skinned
1/2 teaspoon leaf thyme
Salt and freshly ground black pepper to taste

In a large Dutch oven, sauté onion and garlic in the olive oil until onions are lightly browned. Add the wine, thyme, vinegar and salt and pepper. Heap the cabbage in the pan and cook over medium heat for about 15 minutes. (If pan is too full, add cabbage in batches as it cooks down.) Once cabbage is reduced in bulk, tuck the skinned chicken pieces in the cabbage mixture and simmer, covered, about 45 minutes until chicken is tender. Take chicken from pan, remove meat from bones and cut into large pieces. Return chicken pieces to cabbage. Taste for seasonings and correct as necessary. Cool, cover and refrigerate.

About 20 minutes before serving, slowly bring cabbage and chicken to a boil. Transfer to a serving bowl along with some of the sauce.

Serves 6.

Chicken Breasts Bloch

An elegant entree. The pan sauce is delicious spooned over rice. Add the Frosted Consommé to start and the Frozen Lemon Crunch Torte with Raspberry Sauce for dessert for a very impressive dinner.

8-10 boneless chicken breast halves, skin removed
1-1/2 sticks butter
1 cup fine bread crumbs, seasoned to taste with salt, pepper and 1 teaspoon
    basil, crushed
Juice of 1 lemon
2 cloves garlic, minced
2 green onions, finely chopped
1 teaspoon tarragon, crushed, or 1 tablespoon fresh tarragon, minced

Melt butter in small skillet. Dip chicken breasts in melted butter, then cover with bread crumbs, patting the crumbs with the back of a spoon to stick better. Place in one or two glass baking pans, cover with plastic wrap and refrigerate.

Add lemon juice, garlic, chopped onions and tarragon to remaining butter in skillet. Refrigerate.

Two hours before serving, remove chicken and butter/lemon sauce from refrigerator. Reheat sauce and simmer just a minute or two.

Preheat oven to 300 degrees. Pour sauce over chicken and bake, covered with foil, 30 minutes. Remove foil, baste with sauce and bake additional 15 minutes.

Serves 6.

Chicken Lasagne

Pasta, poultry and vegetable all in one dish. Can be refrigerated or frozen. Add a large tossed salad with garbanzo beans, and perhaps Spicy Apple Cake for dessert for a hearty, homey dinner.

8 ounces lasagna noodles
6 chicken breast halves
1 large bunch broccoli
1 pound mushrooms, sliced
1/2 pound sliced baked ham, optional
16 ounces mozzarella cheese, sliced
1/2 cup grated Romano cheese
2 cups chicken broth
1 cup milk
6 tablespoons flour
Salt to taste
1/2 teaspoon ground pepper
1/2 teaspoon ground nutmeg
1 teaspoon marjoram, crushed
1/2 cup grated Parmesan cheese

Cook noodles until al dente as package directs, drain and cool.

Poach chicken breasts 20 minutes in simmering water seasoned with celery stalk, small onion, salt and 3 peppercorns. Remove chicken from broth; reserve broth. Cool chicken and shred into large pieces; set aside, covered.

Remove heavy part of broccoli stalks. Slice remaining stalk and break florets into smaller portions. Parboil in salted water 4 minutes. Drain, rinse with cold water and drain again; set aside.

_____

_____

_____

Melt butter or margarine in small saucepan, whisk in flour, slowly add chicken broth and milk; cook until quite thick. Add salt to taste, ground pepper, nutmeg and marjoram.

In buttered 9 x 13 inch baking dish arrange layer of lasagna noodles, layer of chicken, broccoli, mushrooms, ham, mozzarella cheese, Romano cheese and 1 cup sauce. Repeat layering. Pour remaining sauce over top and sprinkle with Parmesan cheese. Cover with plastic wrap and refrigerate up to two days, or cover tightly with heavy foil and freeze.

Remove from refrigerator a few hours before baking; or remove from freezer to refrigerator 24 hours before baking. Bake in 350-degree oven for 45 minutes.

Serves 6.

Down-Under Golden Nugget Chicken

*A*ttractive, tasty and easy—what more could you ask? An interesting menu could include Ciambotto and toasted pita bread, rice with artichoke hearts and any of the desserts.

Chicken pieces to serve 6
1 package dry onion soup mix
1/2 cup butter or half butter and half margarine
1/2 cup soy sauce
1 teaspoon rosemary, crushed or 2 teaspoons fresh rosemary, chopped
28-ounce can peaches or apricots, drained, juice reserved
1 cup reserved fruit juice
Chopped parsley for garnish

Early in day or evening before serving, wash, dry and trim chicken pieces of excess fat. Place in a single layer in a baking pan.

Melt butter over low heat, add soup mix, soy sauce, rosemary and 1 cup reserved fruit juice. Stir mixture until onion soup is dissolved and heat to boiling. Remove from heat and spoon over chicken.

Cover pan tightly with tin foil and refrigerate.

One hour before baking, remove chicken from refrigerator. Preheat oven to 400 degrees. Bake chicken, uncovered, for 1 hour, basting twice. Add reserved fruit and bake an additional 10 minutes.

Place chicken on a serving platter, arrange fruit attractively and sprinkle with parsley. If your baking dish is suitable, serve from it.

Serves 6.

Hearty Chicken Soup

*H*ere *is an alternative to the Ground Beef Vegetable Garden Soup that we also suggest for a casual supper.*

4 pounds bony chicken parts, wings and backs
2 whole chicken breasts
2-1/2 quarts water
1/2 cup navy beans, parboiled 30 minutes and drained
1-1/2 cups barley
1 tablespoon salt
10 peppercorns
2 bay leaves
4 carrots, peeled and sliced
3 stalks celery with leaves, sliced

1 large onion, chopped
16-ounce can whole tomatoes, coarsely chopped, with juice
1 teaspoon basil, crushed
1 teaspoon marjoram, crushed
1 cup frozen peas
10-ounce box frozen corn kernels
1/4 cup chopped parsley

In large soup kettle place chicken, water, navy beans, barley, salt, peppercorns and bay leaves. Cover kettle and bring to a boil over medium heat. Reduce heat to a simmer and cook 1 hour.

Remove chicken from pot and set aside to cool. Add carrots, celery, tomatoes, basil, marjoram, peas and corn. Cover kettle and return to simmer for 1/2 hour.

When chicken is cool enough to handle, remove meat from bones in bite-size shreds and pieces. Return meat to kettle after vegetables have cooked.

Cool an hour or so before refrigerating. Soup can be stored in the refrigerator for at least a week.

Reheat over low heat, stirring occasionally. Taste for salt and possibly additional herbs while reheating. Add chopped parsley 15 minutes before serving.

Serves 6.

Chicken and Smoked Sausage With Rice

What could be better than a variety of textures and tastes in a one-dish main course. You might like to try the Black Bean Tostados as a first course.

4 chicken breast halves, halved crosswise
6 chicken thighs
1 pound smoked Polish sausage, cut in 2-inch pieces
2 green peppers, sliced vertically
1 sweet red pepper, sliced vertically
10 green onions, sliced into 1/2 inch lengths
4 cloves garlic, minced
4 tomatoes, seeded and coarsely chopped, or 16-ounce can whole tomatoes, drained

3 cups chicken broth, 1 cup reserved
1 cup dry white wine
2 teaspoons salt
1-1/2 tablespoons paprika
1-1/2 teaspoons marjoram
1-1/2 cups long grain rice
1/4 cup chopped parsley for garnish
Oil for browning

Heat oil in large skillet, brown chicken on all sides; set aside.

Brown sausage pieces in same skillet; set aside. If needed, add more oil to skillet before sautéeing peppers and onions. Add garlic, tomatoes, 2 cups chicken broth, wine, salt, paprika and marjoram; scrape up any browned bits in skillet and bring to gentle boil. Add rice, stir together, remove from heat.

Transfer rice and sauce to either a deep 3-quart casserole or a 9 x 13 baking dish. Place chicken pieces and sausage on top. Spoon some sauce over meat. Cool slightly; cover tightly and refrigerate 2 to 3 days.

Remove from refrigerator a few hours before serving. Preheat oven to 325 degrees. Bake covered 45 minutes. After 30 minutes, add additional broth if needed. Stir with a fork. Sprinkle with chopped parsley before serving.

Serves 6.

Turkey Breast Tonnato

This is an economical version of the classic Italian summer dish, Vitello Tonnato.

3-1/2 to 5 pound boneless turkey breast
1 medium onion, chopped
1 large stalk celery, cut in half
1 or 2 bay leaves
6 peppercorns
3/4 cup dry white wine
3 tablespoons melted butter

7-ounce can tuna, drained
2 tablespoons capers, drained
2 tablespoons lemon juice
2 cloves garlic, minced
1/4 cup mayonnaise
Salt to taste
Sliced ripe olives and chopped parsley for garnish

Preheat oven to 325 degrees.

Wash and pat dry turkey breast. Place in an appropriate pan, not on a rack. Add the celery stalk, bay leaves and peppercorns. Mix together the onion, wine and melted butter and pour over the turkey. Roast uncovered 25 minutes per pound, basting several times with the pan juices. Remove turkey from the pan, cool and wrap in plastic wrap, then foil, and refrigerate until you are ready to slice it. Turkey can be prepared up to three days in advance.

Pour pan juices into a measuring cup, scraping up any browned bits from the pan. Remove as much fat as possible and add water as needed to make 1/2 cup.

Transfer to a food processor or blender and whirl until smooth. Add tuna, capers, lemon juice, garlic, tarragon and mayonnaise; whirl until well blended. Taste for salt and add if needed. Pour into a container and refrigerate until 1 hour before serving, stir before using.

Slice cold turkey breast into 1/2-inch slices; arrange overlapping on oblong platter. Spoon ribbon of sauce down center of slices, garnish with sliced olives and parsley. Return to refrigerator until serving time. Transfer remaining sauce to a sauceboat and pass at the table.

Serves 6.

Tarragon Chicken Salad
With Fruit and Nuts

A large glass bowl of this special chicken salad can be the sparkling centerpiece of a casual hot weather dinner that might also include thick slices of red ripe tomatoes lightly dressed with a vinaigrette and fresh basil leaves, sweet white corn on the cob, and ice cream and Oatmeal Lace Cookies for dessert.

8 large chicken breast halves
Olive oil or melted butter as needed
2 cloves garlic, finely minced
Salt and freshly ground black pepper to taste
Juice of half a lemon
1/2 teaspoon curry powder
1 cup best quality mayonnaise
1/4 cup mango chutney
1 tablespoon fresh tarragon leaves or 1/2 tablespoon dried
1 ripe cantaloupe, peeled and cut into 1 inch pieces
1/2 pound seedless green grapes
1 cup walnut halves

Preheat oven to 375 degrees. Place chicken breasts, skin side up, on a large baking sheet. Brush skin with oil or melted butter, sprinkle minced garlic on top and season well with salt and pepper. Bake chicken until well browned, 30-45 minutes. When cool enough to handle, remove skin and bones. Cut meat into 1-inch pieces.

In serving bowl, toss chicken with the mayonnaise, lemon juice, curry powder, chutney, tarragon, cantaloupe and grapes, and more salt to taste. Cover and chill well, then taste again for seasonings and adjust as necessary. Just before serving, toss again with the walnut halves.

Serves 6.

Jambalaya

*One of the many versions of this Southern favorite. Hearty and soul satis-
fying, our zippy rice and sausage casserole could be served with a crisp
green salad and French bread. Light first and final courses hit the right
note.*

18 best quality small link sausages
1 pound boneless and skinless chicken
   breasts
1 large onion, diced
1 large green pepper, diced
2 garlic cloves, minced
28-ounce can tomatoes
1 can sliced okra, drained

2 cups chicken stock (reserve one cup)
2 tablespoons chili powder
1/4 teaspoon leaf thyme
1 bay leaf
Salt and freshly ground black pepper to
   taste
2 cups long grain rice

In flame-proof serving casserole, cook sausages until nicely browned;
remove from pan and drain. Reserve. Spoon out all but three tablespoons
of sausage fat from pan. Cut chicken breasts into bite-size pieces. Sauté
in sausage fat until lightly browned, about five minutes. Remove from
pan and add to sausages.

Briefly sauté onion, garlic and green pepper in same pan, until onion is
translucent. Add tomatoes, okra, 1 cup of the chicken stock, seasonings,
sausage and chicken to pan, and simmer mixture about 15 minutes.
Taste for seasonings and adjust as necesssary. Let cool, then cover and
refrigerate until 45 minutes before serving.

Preheat oven to 375 degrees. Slowly bring sausage mixture to a boil on
top of the stove, add the rice and stir. Cover and bake in oven about 30
minutes, until liquid is absorbed and rice is cooked. If mixture becomes
too dry before rice is cooked, add hot stock a scant quarter cup at a time;
the rice should not be mushy. Remove bay leaf before serving.

Serves 6.

Italian Sausage, Shrimp and Rice Casserole

This combination of flavors will enliven everyone's palate. Start with a first course of Marinated Green Bean and Zucchini Salad and for dessert, a simple Pound Cake with Lemon Glaze, or your favorite fruit.

1 pound sweet Italian sausages, with fennel if available

8 green onions, sliced

1/2 pound mushrooms, sliced

2 cloves garlic, minced

1/2 pound ham steak, cubed

3 tablespoons flour

3 tablespoons butter

1-1/2 cups raw long grain rice

16-ounce can plum tomatoes, coarsely chopped, and their juice

1/2 cup dry white wine

1 cup water

1/2 teaspoon basil, crushed

1/4 teaspoon Tabasco, or to taste

1 teaspoon salt

1/2 teaspoon fennel seeds, if not in sausage (optional)

1 pound medium shelled and deveined raw shrimp

1/2 cup chicken broth

Remove casings from sausages and slice sausage into 1/2 to 1 inch pieces. Add sausage to 3-quart Dutch oven or large skillet and lightly brown, stirring occasionally. Add sliced green onions, mushrooms and garlic. Cook over medium heat, 3 to 5 minutes. Dredge cubed ham in flour and add with 3 tablespoons butter to casserole or skillet. Cook 2 to 3 minutes over low heat.

Add rice, tomatoes, wine, water, basil, Tabasco, salt, and fennel seeds. Bring to a boil, reduce heat to low and cook, covered, about 15 minutes.

Add shrimp and part of chicken broth if mixture seems dry. Cook 3 minutes more, until shrimp turns pink.

Cool casserole or remove ingredients from skillet to serving casserole, cover tightly and refrigerate up to 2 days before serving.

Remove from refrigerator about 2 hours before baking. Add more chicken broth as needed. Bake in preheated 325-degree oven 30 to 40 minutes, covered.

Serves 6.

Sausage and Cous Cous

A slightly exotic entree for a meal that could start with cured olives, string cheese and pistachios, and end with Figs Poached in Red Wine.

18 small links (about 2-1/2 pounds) hot Italian sausage (veal sausage if available)

1 pound carrots, scraped and cut into 2-inch pieces

1 pound green beans, trimmed and sliced in half on the diagonal

16-ounce can Italian plum tomatoes

1 large onion, sliced

1/4 teaspoon cumin

1/4 teaspoon ground coriander

1/4 teaspoon thyme

2 tablespoons olive oil

1/4 cup currants

16-ounce can chick peas, rinsed and drained

3 cups water or chicken broth

1-1/2 cups cous cous

1 teaspoon salt

2 tablespoons butter

Small can of harissa (Middle Eastern hot sauce) or Tabasco-type sauce

Sauté sliced onions in the olive oil until translucent. Add carrots, currants, chick peas, cumin, coriander, thyme, and canned tomatoes. Simmer, covered, for 20 minutes, stirring occasionally.

Add sausage links, cover and simmer for another 20 minutes, stirring the sausages into the sauce. Add the green beans, cover and simmer another 20 minutes.

Let cool, then cover and chill overnight. Remove most of the congealed sausage grease. About 30 minutes before serving, slowly reheat until very hot, stirring from time to time.

About 15 minutes before serving, bring the water or broth, butter and salt to a boil. Remove from heat, add cous cous, stir and cover. Let cous cous sit about 10 minutes or until all liquid is absorbed; fluff with a fork.

Turn cous cous into large, shallow serving bowl and make a well in the center. Fill with the sausage and vegetable mixture and a spoonful of the broth. Pass the hot sauce for those who like their food really spicy.

Serves 6.

Baked Sausages and Vegetables

This is one of those almost embarrassingly easy recipes that nonetheless makes a great party dish—plenty of flavor and color. Start the meal with a cheese dish, serve the casserole with crusty bread, red wine and a green salad, and end with a light fruit dessert.

18 best quality fresh sausage links, such as Italian or lamb, about 2-1/2 pounds

18 small round new potatoes, red skinned if available, scrubbed

18 small white onions, peeled, or 6 leeks, cleaned and halved with a small amount of the green left on

12 carrots, about the same size, scraped and cut into 2-inch pieces

1 large bulb fennel, cleaned, trimmed and cut into 2-inch pieces

2 large red peppers, seeded and cut into sixths

2 large green peppers, seeded and cut into sixths

4 tablespoons olive oil

1 teaspoon rosemary leaves or Italian seasoning

Salt and pepper to taste

1/4 cup finely minced parsley

In a large shallow baking dish, mix the potatoes, carrots, onions or leeks, and fennel with the olive oil, rosemary or Italian seasoning, and salt and pepper. Spread in one layer. Cover with plastic wrap and refrigerate until 1 hour before serving.

Prick sausages, then place on a rack in a second large baking dish, cover and refrigerate as above. Place the sliced peppers in a plastic bag until one hour before serving.

About one hour before dinner, place root vegetables, uncovered, in a preheated 400-degree oven. About 30 minutes before serving, add the pan of sausages, uncovered, to the oven. Stir the vegetables carefully. About 15 minutes before serving, add the peppers to the other vegetables, mixing gently.

When potatoes can be easily pierced with a fork, combine sausages and vegetables in a large white serving bowl, distributing the colors artfully. Sprinkle with parsley.

Serves 6.

White Bean Casserole

With a pot of home-cooked beans on hand, you have the base for any number of delicious favorites: cassoulet, roast leg of lamb with beans, bean purée, bean salad, bean soup. Here, the well-flavored beans are topped with Polish sausage (kielbasa), and baked until both beans and meat are crusty on the outside, yet juicy and tender within.

3 cups (1-1/2 pounds) dried white beans, picked over and washed

Water to cover

3 cloves garlic, minced

1 large onion, finely chopped

2 teaspoons salt and lots of freshly ground black pepper

One stalk celery, chopped fine; 2 cloves; 2 carrots peeled and chopped fine; one bay leaf; 4 sprigs parsley, chopped fine; 1/2 teaspoon dried thyme, all tied together in cheesecloth

16-ounce can cooking tomatoes, chopped

1 cup seasoned breadcrumbs

Chicken broth or water

2-1/2 pounds kielbasa, in one long sausage if possible

1/2 cup minced parsley for garnish

Cover the beans with water and let stand overnight. The next day, drain off any leftover water. Place beans in a large kettle, and add the garlic, onions, seasonings tied in cheesecloth, salt, pepper, and the tomatoes. Add enough broth or water to cover by an inch or so. Simmer for about 45 to 60 minutes, until beans are tender but not mushy. Discard cheesecloth bag, and adjust seasonings.

Transfer the beans and some of their broth to a large round or oval casserole about 2 inches deep. Top with the breadcrumbs. Reserve leftover broth. Score the sausage link on the diagonal about every 3 inches. Roll into a round or oval and place on beans. Cover and refrigerate up to two days in advance.

About 45 minutes before dinner, place uncovered casserole in a preheated 375-degree oven and bake until bubbly and crusty. Add more broth if needed. Sprinkle with the chopped parsley.

Serves 6.

Sausage and Peppers

Turn this old favorite into a company dish by serving it with polenta—Italian cornmeal mush. For lump-free polenta, blend the cornmeal with one-third the amount of water called for in your recipe, then add mixture slowly to the rest of the water, which you have brought to a boil, stirring constantly. Reduce heat to a simmer and cook until very thick, stirring frequently. (Try instant polenta if you can find it.) Leftover polenta is delicious sliced and sautéed in olive oil or butter!

28-ounce can Italian plum tomatoes
3 tablespoons olive oil
3 cloves garlic, minced
3 large onions, peeled, halved and thinly sliced
18 links best quality hot Italian sausage, about 2-1/2 pounds
6 large green sweet peppers, seeded and sliced in long, thin strips
(NOTE: The sausages provide all the seasonings necessary.)

In a large casserole or Dutch oven, cook onion slices and garlic in olive oil until transparent. Do not brown.

Carefully add the plum tomatoes, chopping them up with a spoon. Cook uncovered over medium heat, stirring occasionally, for about 20 minutes.

Place sausages in the tomato sauce and pile the peppers on top. (Peppers will cook down.) Bring mixture to a boil, reduce heat to a simmer and cover pot. As peppers cook down, stir into sauce. Cook at the simmer until sausages are well done, about 25 minutes.

If you are not serving immediately, let mixture cool, then refrigerate overnight. Remove as much of the congealed grease as possible. Reheat slowly until very hot, stirring from time to time.

Serves 6.

Spinach Lasagne

This satisfying casserole is great for your vegetarian guests. It freezes well and tastes best when the flavors have been allowed to blend.

1 pound lasagne noodles, cooked until al dente and drained (To prevent the noodles from sticking together, mix very gently after draining with 1 tablespoon olive oil)

2 boxes frozen chopped spinach, thawed and squeezed dry

16-ounce carton ricotta or small curd cottage cheese

3 eggs

1/8 teaspoon ground nutmeg

1 pound whole milk mozzarella, grated

1 cup freshly grated Parmesan cheese

Salt and freshly ground black pepper to taste

28-ounce can Italian plum tomatoes

3 tablespoons olive oil

3 cloves garlic, peeled and lightly smashed

3 dried hot red peppers

In a medium saucepan, heat the olive oil, then add garlic and hot peppers, brown both well and discard. Carefully add the tomatoes, and simmer about 20 minutes, stirring occasionally to chop the tomatoes. Let cool.

In a large mixing bowl, beat the eggs well. Add the chopped spinach, the ricotta or cottage cheese, the nutmeg, about 1/4 cup of the Parmesan cheese and salt and pepper to taste.

To assemble, distribute about 1/2 cup of the tomato sauce over the bottom of a 9 x 13-inch baking dish. Add a layer of noodles, then a layer of the cheese and spinach mixture, then a layer of the grated mozzarella, more tomato sauce, and sprinkle with Parmesan. Repeat until pan is almost full. End with tomato sauce and a good dusting of Parmesan. Cover with foil and refrigerate up to 3 days or freeze.

Bring lasagne to room temperature. Bake, uncovered, on a cookie sheet at 375 degrees, approximately one hour. Let rest briefly, then cut into squares.

Serves 6.

Seaside Fettuccine

*H*ere is a versatile pasta sauce that is equally good hot or cold depending on the season. The Zucchini and Basil Soup is a good first course as it can also be served hot or cold.

12 ounces fettuccine, cooked al dente
1 pound firm fish fillets
1/2 pound small shrimp, peeled
6 fresh tomatoes (use only summer-ripe tomatoes) or 16-ounce can Italian plum tomatoes, drained
1/2 cup olive oil
1 large onion, chopped

3 cloves garlic, minced
1/4 cup dry white wine
1-1/2 teaspoons basil, crushed, or 1 tablespoon fresh, chopped
1 teaspoon marjoram or 2 teaspoons fresh
1 teaspoon salt, or to taste
1/2 teaspoon freshly ground pepper
1/2 cup chopped parsley

Poach fish in lightly salted, simmering water 3 minutes; break into large flakes and set aside.

Sauté onion in hot olive oil until just wilted, add garlic and cook briefly.

Add tomatoes, coarsely chopped, wine and herbs to onion and garlic mixture and simmer about 10 minutes. Add shrimp and simmer an additional 5 minutes.

Remove from heat and gently stir in flaked fish. Transfer to a bowl, cover and refrigerate up to one day before serving. If serving hot, place sauce in large skillet and just heat through over low heat. Spoon over fettuccine cooked as follows: Bring large pot of salted water to a boil before guests arrive. Turn off heat and keep covered. At appropriate time before serving, bring back to boil, add pasta, cook about 5 minutes; drain, toss with 1 tablespoon olive oil, return to pot and keep covered until first course has been finished.

When serving cold bring sauce and fettuccine to room temperature before serving. Fettuccine can be cooked the day before, tossed with 1 tablespoon olive oil, covered tightly, and refrigerated. Serve in a large shallow bowl.

Serves 6.

Crumb-Topped Baked Fish Fillets

This is one of the few fish entrees that can be prepared successfully early in the day, then popped into the oven before sitting down to the first course. For an elegant finish, try the Frozen Lemon Crunch Torte with Raspberry Sauce.

3 pounds firm fish fillets, such as cod, haddock, sea bass
Salt to sprinkle over fish
1/8 teaspoon pepper
2-1/2 cups fresh cracked wheat bread crumbs, about 6 slices
1 teaspoon salt
1/2 teaspoon garlic powder
1 teaspoon marjoram, crushed
1/2 teaspoon rosemary, crumbled
2 tablespoons chopped parsley
1/2 cup grated Swiss cheese
1/2 cup melted butter
Butter for baking dish

Wash and pat dry fillets. Place in 1 or 2 buttered shallow baking pans. Sprinkle with salt and pepper. Mix together bread crumbs, salt, garlic powder, marjoram, rosemary, parsley and Swiss cheese. Add melted butter and toss together.

Pat seasoned crumbs evenly over fish. Cover with plastic wrap and refrigerate. Remove from refrigerator 1/2 hour before baking. Preheat oven to 350 degrees. Bake uncovered 20 to 25 minutes. Serve with lemon wedges.

Serves 6.

Ossobuco (Braised Veal Shanks)

Veal shanks cooked in a well-flavored sauce are an all-too-rare treat. If veal shanks rarely appear in your market, buy them whenever you see them, wrap well and store in the freezer until you have enough for a meal. Risotto is the classic Italian accompaniment for ossobuco, although plain white rice or flat buttered noodles will do nicely.

6 large, meaty veal shanks
Flour
Salt and freshly ground black pepper to taste
6 tablespoons olive oil
1 16-ounce can tomatoes, chopped
1 cup dry white wine (dry vermouth is fine)
1 cup chicken broth as needed

1 bay leaf
1/4 teaspoon thyme
4 small anchovy fillets
2 cloves of garlic, peeled
6 sprigs fresh parsley, tough stems removed
4 thin slices of lemon peel, white pith removed

Mince together last four ingredients until finely mixed; set aside. In a brown paper bag, shake the shanks with flour and salt and pepper until shanks are well coated. Brown the shanks well in the oil. Pour the tomatoes, white wine, bay leaf, thyme and reserved seasonings over the browned shanks, and stir. Cool, cover and refrigerate.

About 1 hour before serving, slowly reheat shanks until boiling, then lower heat and simmer, covered, for about 50 minutes or until meat is fork tender. Turn gently once or twice to distribute seasonings. Add chicken broth as necessary to keep shanks almost covered.

Remove shanks to a serving platter. Taste sauce for seasoning and adjust if necessary. If sauce is too thin, boil it uncovered until slightly thickened; pour over shanks.

Serves 6.

Pasta and Veal Victoria

A complete meal in one dish. Freezes well.

12 ounces linguine
1 pound ground veal
1 cup finely chopped onions
1/2 cup finely chopped carrots
1/2 cup finely chopped celery
9 tablespoons butter, divided
10-3/4-ounce can chicken broth
1 teaspoon tarragon, crushed
1 teaspoon salt
1/2 teaspoon ground pepper

1 pound mushrooms, thinly sliced and
    tossed with 2 tablespoons lemon juice
4 tablespoons flour
1-1/2 cups milk
1 cup light cream
1 teaspoon salt
1/4 teaspoon ground pepper
1/4 teaspoon ground nutmeg
1 cup frozen peas, defrosted
1/2 cup freshly grated Parmesan cheese

Sauté onions, carrots and celery in 4 tablespoons butter in large skillet until golden. Add veal and brown. Stir in broth, tarragon, salt and pepper and simmer, partially covered, for 20 minutes. Cook linguine until al dente, drain and toss with 1 tablespoon salad oil to prevent sticking; set aside. Sauté mushrooms in 2 tablespoons butter over high heat in a large skillet; transfer to a bowl. Melt remaining butter in same skillet over low heat. Add flour and cook 1 minute. Whisk in milk and cream, and cook over medium heat until thick. Reduce heat, add salt, pepper, nutmeg, mushrooms and peas; simmer about 5 minutes.

Spread 1/3 meat sauce in bottom of 7 x 11 baking dish. Top with 1/2 linguine. Continue with 1/3 meat sauce, 1/2 cream sauce, remaining linguine, remaining meat sauce, then cream sauce. Sprinkle with Parmesan. Cool, cover with foil. Refrigerate up to 2 days or freeze. Defrost in refrigerator overnight, remove from refrigerator 2 hours before baking. Preheat oven to 350 degrees; bake, covered, 45 minutes. Remove cover and bake additional 15 minutes.

Serves 6.

Veal Stew With Tiny Peas and Mushrooms

Veal stew is a welcome treat any time of the year. In the summer, try it with fresh tomato slices dressed in a dill vinaigrette, or when tomatoes are not in season, with baked cherry tomatoes sprinkled with dill, salt and pepper, and olive oil and baked in a hot oven until just heated through. If you add sour cream to the stew, serve flat buttered noodles; if not, serve great French bread to dip in the sauce.

3 pounds veal stew meat, cut in 1-1/2 inch cubes
1/3 cup flour
Salt and freshly ground pepper to taste
4 tablespoons olive oil
1 cup chicken stock
1/2 cup dry white wine
2 tablespoons tomato paste
1/2 pound large fresh mushroom caps, cleaned and cut into quarters (reserve
    stems for another use)
1 box frozen tiny peas (petit pois)
1/2 teaspoon sage leaves
2 cloves garlic, minced
3/4 cup sour cream (optional)

In a brown paper bag, shake together the veal cubes, flour and salt and pepper, until the veal is well coated. Sauté the veal in the olive oil until nicely browned. Place the browned veal in a Dutch oven, and add the chicken stock, white wine, tomato paste, sage and minced garlic. Cover and bring to a boil. Uncover and reduce heat; simmer, stirring often, until veal is almost tender, 30-40 minutes. Add the mushrooms and cook 10 minutes longer. Add the frozen peas and cook for five minutes more. Taste for seasonings and adjust as necessary. Let cool, cover and refrigerate.

About 20 minutes before serving, reheat slowly to boiling, stirring from time to time. When stew is hot, add the sour cream if you are using it but do not let stew boil again.

Serves 6.

Fruited Lamb Curry

Sometimes it's fun to serve as many curry accompaniments as you can come up with, from sweet to savory. A somewhat less hectic approach is the one we take here: the curry has fruit and chutney already in it, so you may want to confine the side dishes to some more chutney and perhaps grated coconut. Serve with plain white rice.

3 pounds lamb shoulder, cut in 1-1/2 inch cubes
1 large onion, chopped
3 cloves garlic, minced
3 to 4 tablespoons vegetable oil
Salt and freshly ground black pepper to taste
3 to 4 tablespoons curry powder
1 cup chicken stock
1/2 cup currants
16-ounce can of pineapple chunks in juice, well drained
1 tart apple, seeded and cubed
2 bananas
1/2 cup chutney
1 cup yogurt

In a large Dutch oven, brown the lamb cubes in the oil; remove with a slotted spoon. Spoon off all but 1 tablespoon of the oil, add the onion and garlic and sauté briefly. Put the lamb back in the casserole, add the curry powder and salt and pepper to taste. Stir. Add the chicken stock, currants, pineapple chunks and the chutney. Bring mixture to a boil, then simmer, covered, until tender (about 45 minutes), stirring from time to time. Stir in the cup of yogurt and the apple. Taste for seasonings and adjust as necessary. Cool, cover and refrigerate.

At serving time, reheat very slowly, stirring occasionally, until very hot. Just before putting the curry in a serving bowl, slice the two bananas into it.

Serves 6.

Lamb Shanks With Orzo

An earthy peasant dish for a crowd. Orzo—rice-shaped pasta—is available in many large supermarkets and at Greek and Italian food markets.

6 large meaty lamb shanks, or 3 pounds lamb stewing meat, cut into 1-1/2 inch cubes

Flour, about 1/2 cup

Salt and freshly ground black pepper to taste

3 tablespoons olive oil

3 cloves garlic, minced

1 large onion, peeled and diced

3 stalks celery, diced

1 large green pepper, seeded and diced

16-ounce can Italian plum tomatoes

1/2 cup dry white wine (dry vermouth is fine)

1 or more cups canned or homemade chicken broth

1 bay leaf

1 tablespoon rosemary leaves

3 dashes hot pepper sauce

8 ounces orzo

In a brown paper bag, shake the lamb with the flour and salt and pepper until well coated. In a skillet, brown the lamb well on all sides in the olive oil. Add the chopped vegetables and cook, stirring, until the onions are translucent. Transfer all ingredients to a Dutch oven or flameproof casserole with a lid. Add the tomatoes, with their juice, the wine, bay leaf, and rosemary, and the hot pepper sauce if desired. Bring to a boil, then lower heat and simmer until lamb is tender, about 1 hour. Taste for salt and add more if necessary.

Cool, cover and refrigerate until 2 hours before serving. Bring stew to room temperature.

Preheat oven to 400 degrees. Reheat lamb mixture slowly on top of stove until boiling, about 15 minutes. Add the orzo and 1 cup chicken broth. Bring to boil again. Cover and place in oven for about 10 to 15 minutes until orzo is "al dente"—or cooked through but firm to the bite. Add more broth as necessary. Remove bay leaf. Serve from the casserole or place orzo, vegetables (and a little broth, if desired) in a large shallow serving dish and place lamb on top.

Serves 6.

Moroccan Lamb Stew

This stew could be considered "heavy," so plan a lighter first course and maybe a simple dessert from the Fresh Fruit Compendium. To accompany the stew, try bulgur wheat or brown rice.

3 pounds cubed leg of lamb
Salad oil for browning
4 tablespoons butter or margarine
1/2 cup flour
1 tablespoon salt
1/2 teaspoon pepper
1 cup chopped onions
4 cloves garlic, minced
Grated orange peel of 2 oranges
2 teaspoons dried thyme, crushed

1 teaspoon cumin seeds
2 teaspoons dried rosemary
2 bay leaves
2 cups chicken broth
Juice of 2 oranges
12 pitted prunes, halved
8 dried figs, halved
1/2 cup slivered almonds, toasted
Chopped parsley for garnish

Trim meat of fat and gristle, pat dry. Mix flour with salt and pepper in shallow bowl, dredge lamb. Heat oil in Dutch oven over medium-high heat, brown a single layer of lamb on all sides, set aside; repeat until all meat is browned.

Melt butter over medium heat in same pot, add onions, cook until limp and lightly browned. Add garlic, orange rind, thyme, cumin, rosemary and bay leaves, heat for about 1 minute, until fragrant, stirring constantly. Return lamb to Dutch oven, add broth and orange juice, stir together, bring to gentle boil. Cover and place in preheated 325-degree oven for 1 hour. Remove from oven, cool and refrigerate or freeze until ready to serve. If frozen, thaw overnight in refrigerator; bring to almost room temperature before reheating.

Preheat oven to 325 degrees; add prunes, figs and almonds to stew and heat in oven about 30 minutes. Remove bay leaves. Transfer to serving bowl and sprinkle with chopped parsley.

Serves 6.

Company Lamb Loaf
With Yogurt Dill Sauce

*H*ere is a meat loaf worthy of the most special guests.

2 pounds ground lamb
3 tablespoons butter
1 cup chopped onion
3 cloves garlic, chopped
1/4 cup chopped green pepper
2 eggs
1/2 cup milk
2 slices fresh white bread
1/4 cup chopped fresh dill or 1 tablespoon dried dillweed
1 tablespoon chopped parsley
1/2 teaspoon oregano, crushed
1/2 teaspoon ground allspice or combine cinnamon, ground cloves and nutmeg

1/2 teaspoon cinnamon
1/2 teaspoon cardamom
1-1/2 teaspoons salt
1/2 teaspoon ground pepper
Grated lemon peel from 1 lemon

Yogurt Dill Sauce
1-1/2 cups plain yogurt
1 tablespoon chopped fresh dill or 1 teaspoon dried dillweed
1 tablespoon chopped parsley
1/2 teaspoon salt
1/4 teaspoon freshly ground pepper

Melt butter over medium heat in a skillet; sauté onion, garlic and green pepper until limp.

In a large bowl, whisk egg and milk, add bread to soak a couple of minutes. Add ground lamb and mix together. Add sautéed onion, garlic and green pepper mixture, dill, parsley, oregano, allspice, cinnamon, cardamom, salt, pepper and lemon peel. Mix thoroughly. Shape into oblong loaf and wrap in plastic wrap and then foil. Freeze until day before serving.

Thaw loaf in refrigerator overnight. Preheat oven to 350 degrees 1-1/2 hours before serving. Bake loaf one hour and 15 minutes. Drain grease and place loaf on serving platter; allow to set about ten minutes before slicing. Lightly cover with foil to keep warm.

Combine all ingredients for Yogurt Dill Sauce; pass separately.

Serves 6.

Ground Beef Vegetable Garden Soup

An annual favorite party is our Sunday Soup Supper where "casual" is the password. Serve an assortment of finger-type appetizers followed by this hearty soup and a basket of crusty breads. For dessert, heat up from the freezer Butter Crust Apple Kuchen.

2 pounds lean ground beef (not ground round)
2 large onions, halved and sliced
3 quarts water
3/4 cup lentils
1 tablespoon salt
28-ounce can whole tomatoes, broken up
2 large stalks celery, sliced
3 carrots, sliced
2 medium zucchini, sliced
1/2 small head cabbage, coarsely chopped
1/2 cup chopped green pepper

1/2 cup raw rice
2 garlic cloves, minced
2 beef boullion cubes
2 teaspoons chili powder
1 teaspoon basil, crushed
1 teaspoon oregano, crushed
1 teaspoon caraway seeds
1 teaspoon celery seeds
2 teaspoons sugar
16-ounce can whole kernel corn, drained

In large soup pot or Dutch oven, brown meat and sliced onions. Add water, lentils and salt; cover and simmer for about 1 hour.

Add tomatoes, celery, carrots, green pepper, rice, garlic, boullion cubes, chili powder, basil, oregano, caraway seeds, celery seeds and sugar. Bring back to a simmer and cook covered about 30 minutes. Add zucchini, cabbage and corn and return to simmer, uncovered, for 15 minutes.

Cool soup, cover and refrigerate for up to 1 week before serving.

Bring to room temperature and reheat over very low heat. Taste for seasonings and adjust to taste.

Serves 6.

Stuffed Beef Roll, Hot or Cold

*H*ere is an interesting entree that is equally suitable for either warm or cold weather dining.

3 to 4 pound eye of round roast
2 sweet Italian sausages
6-ounce package cooked ham, diced
1 medium onion, chopped
1/2 cup chopped green pepper
2 cloves garlic, minced
1/2 teaspoon basil, crushed
1/2 teaspoon salt

1/4 teaspoon ground pepper
1 teaspoon paprika
3 tablespoons bacon drippings or salad oil
   for browning
1 cup hot water
6 whole cloves
1 large bay leaf
3 slices bacon

With a long sharp knife make a crescent-shaped cut lengthwise through the middle of the roast. Combine sausage, ham, onion, green pepper, garlic and basil, and stuff into cut in roast, packing well. Close ends with toothpicks or skewers. Rub roast with mixture of salt, pepper and paprika. Heat drippings or oil in skillet and brown roast on all sides. Transfer to roasting pan. Add hot water and seasonings, lay bacon on top lengthwise. Cover tightly with foil. Bake in 325-degree oven for 30 minutes per pound, basting occasionally. Remove from pan, cool and wrap meat well. Pour sauce through sieve and store roast and sauce separately for up to 3 days.

To serve cold, slice meat in 1/2-inch slices and arrange attractively on serving platter. Use gravy as base for soup. Or, if you are fond of aspic, dissolve plain gelatin (1 package) in water, add canned beef broth to gravy to make 2 cups. Pour into square pan, refrigerate until set. Cut into cubes and place on platter with sliced roast.

To serve roast hot, slice up to 2 hours before reheating. Arrange slices in oblong baking dish, pour gravy on top and cover loosely with foil. Reheat in preheated 325-degree oven for 30 minutes. Serve in baking dish sprinkled with chopped parsley or transfer with wide spatula to serving platter. Serve gravy on the side.

Serves 6.

Baked Spiced Corned Beef

*H*ere is a special company version of an old favorite, corned beef, but without the boiled cabbage and potatoes. You might like to serve the Layered Vegetable Pâté as a first course and the Potato and Fruit Gratin as a side dish.

3-4 pound corned beef brisket or round
3 tablespoons pickling spice
1 medium onion, sliced
1 orange, sliced

1 stalk celery, cut into 3-inch pieces
1 carrot, scraped and cut into 2-inch pieces
1/2 cup brown sugar
1 tablespoon dry mustard

Soak corned beef in cold water for 1/2 hour. Place long sheet of heavy-duty foil in a shallow baking pan. Remove meat from water to center of foil. Sprinkle on pickling spice, then scatter sliced onions, oranges and celery and carrot pieces on and around meat. Mix brown sugar and dry mustard and sprinkle over meat. Bring ends of foil up over meat and seal tightly.

Bake in preheated 325-degree oven for three hours. Open foil carefully, remove meat to platter and cover lightly until cool.

Strain meat sauce through a sieve, pressing solids with the back of a spoon. Cover and refrigerate or freeze.

When meat is cool, slice across the grain in rather thin slices. Wrap tightly in foil and refrigerate for several days or freeze up to two weeks.

Thaw frozen meat and sauce in refrigerator overnight. Arrange meat in shallow baking dish that can be brought to the table. Pour some of the sauce over meat and cover lightly with foil so that it doesn't steam. Heat in preheated 325-degree oven 20 minutes.

Heat remaining meat sauce separately and pass in a sauce boat at the table.

Serves 6.

Stifado (Greek Beef Stew)

This rich and delicious stew, touched with cinnamon, is an excellent winter choice. You might start with Bourekas (phyllo triangles filled with cheese), serve the stew with Chick Pea Salad and Greek bread, and end the meal with Low-Calorie Lemon Mousse.

3 tablespoons olive oil
3 pounds beef stew meat, cut into 2-inch cubes
2 12-ounce bags frozen tiny onions
4 cloves garlic, minced
1/2 of a 6-ounce can of tomato paste
1 cup dry red wine
1/4 cup red wine vinegar
1 bay leaf, 1 cinnamon stick or 1/2 teaspoon ground cinnamon and 2 whole cloves, tied together in cheesecloth
1/2 teaspoon ground cumin
1 teaspoon rosemary
2 tablespoons brown sugar
Salt and freshly ground black pepper to taste
1 cup water or beef stock, as needed

In a large Dutch oven or flameproof casserole, brown the beef cubes in the olive oil. Spoon off any excess oil. Mix onions and garlic with the browned beef.

In a small bowl, combine the rest of ingredients until well blended. Pour over beef mixture and stir thoroughly. Bring mixture to a boil, then reduce to a simmer. Cover. Simmer for about 1 hour or until beef is tender, stirring occasionally. Add water or broth if needed. Cool, cover and refrigerate until 1 hour before serving.

Reheat over low flame until very hot; stir from time to time. Remove cheesecloth containing cinnamon stick, cloves and bay leaf before serving.

Serves 6.

Oriental Beef Stew

Satisfy your desire for a Chinese-style dinner without the last-minute stir-frying. Vegetables Vinaigrette #5 from our side dish section would be a colorful addition.

3 pounds beef chuck, trimmed of gristle and cut into 1-1/2 inch cubes
5 tablespoons salad oil, divided
1 tablespoon minced ginger root, about a 1-inch piece
4 cloves garlic, minced
1/2 teaspoon red pepper flakes
2 large onions, halved and sliced
14-1/2 ounce can plum tomatoes, undrained and coarsely chopped
1/3 cup soy sauce
1/3 cup smooth peanut butter
Unsalted roasted peanuts, chopped, for garnish

Over medium flame, heat 3 tablespoons oil in 3-quart Dutch oven; add ginger root, garlic and pepper flakes, cook just until fragrant. Turn heat to high, add layer of meat and sear on all sides, remove with slotted spoon and repeat until all is browned.

Add remaining oil and sliced onions to pot, cook until onions are limp and slightly golden. Add tomatoes, soy sauce and browned meat to pot, cover, bring to a boil, reduce heat and simmer about 1-1/2 hours. Stir in peanut butter and simmer a few minutes. Cool the stew and refrigerate up to 3 days, or freeze.

Bring to room temperature. Reheat in covered Dutch oven over low heat about 30 minutes before serving, or preheat oven to 325 degrees and reheat, covered, about 30 minutes. With either method, stir occasionally.

Transfer to serving bowl, and sprinkle with chopped peanuts.

Serves 6.

Linguine and
Meat Sauce Norwood

The story goes that this "spaghetti" sauce, passed down through the family, was created by a Greek gentleman. His secret ingredient might be the chili powder. In any event, we are grateful to him. Sauce freezes well.

2 pounds ground chuck
3 cloves garlic, minced
3 onions, diced
2 green peppers, diced
3 stalks celery, diced
1/4 pound mushrooms, cleaned and sliced
1/4 cup parsley, minced
2-3 tablespoons chili powder
Salt and freshly ground black pepper to taste
28-ounce can Italian plum tomatoes
6-ounce can tomato paste and 1 can water
1-1/2 pounds linguine

In a Dutch oven, brown chuck, stirring to break up large lumps. Drain well. Stir in chili powder and salt and pepper and cook briefly. Add vegetables, tomato paste and water. Blend well. Bring mixture to a boil, then reduce to a slow simmer. Simmer, covered, about 45 minutes, stirring occasionally. Taste for salt and chili powder and add more if necessary. The sauce should have a rich taste and a spicy ending, with the chopped vegetables cooked through but not mushy. Cool, cover and refrigerate or freeze.

At serving time, slowly reheat sauce. Bring a large pot of salted water to the boil and add linguine in handfuls; after water returns to the boil, cook linguine about 7 minutes or until al dente. Drain well. In a large shallow serving bowl, mix noodles and 3 cups of the sauce. Serve at table. Pass the remaining sauce in a separate bowl.

Serves 6.

Pork Carbonnade

Like most stews, this one improves after spending a few days in the refrigerator awaiting the party. The rich gravy is terrific over homemade spaetzles (little dumplings) or egg noodles sprinkled with caraway seeds. Try one of our many fruit desserts for the finale.

1/2 pound thick bacon cut into 1-inch pieces
2 tablespoons vegetable oil
2-1/2 pounds boneless pork loin, cut into 1-1/2 inch cubes
1/2 cup flour
1-1/2 teaspoons salt
1/2 teaspoon pepper
2 large onions, halved and thinly sliced
3 cloves garlic, minced

3 tablespoons flour
10-1/2 ounce can beef stock
2 cups dark beer (like Dos Equis or Becks)
2 tablespoons vinegar
1 heaping tablespoon brown sugar
1/2 teaspoon thyme
1 teaspoon rosemary, crumbled

Sauté the bacon pieces in a large heavy casserole. When rendered of fat, remove and reserve. Add vegetable oil to the casserole and heat.

Dredge the cubed pork in the seasoned flour and brown on high heat. Do not crowd the meat as it will steam and not brown properly; brown in two or more batches if necessary. Set meat aside after browning. Add sliced onions and garlic to remaining fat and cook over low heat until limp and golden. Sprinkle flour on top and cook briefly. Slowly stir in beef broth and beer and cook until thickened. Add vinegar, sugar and herbs and simmer about 3 or 4 minutes. Add reserved bacon and pork cubes and mix.

Cover casserole and place in preheated 350-degree oven. Bake for 1 hour. Cool about an hour before storing in the refrigerator up to two days before serving.

Remove from refrigerator at least one hour before heating in a 325-degree preheated oven for 45 minutes. Taste for seasonings after 30 minutes and adjust to taste.

Serves 6.

Roast Pork With Game Sauce

This roast is a nice alternative to cold poached chicken breasts for a summer menu, but it is just as tasty served hot for cold weather entertaining. Cherry Tomatoes with Parsley Pesto for a first course and the Cracker Crust Pecan Pie with Mocha Cream are some suggested accompaniments.

2-1/2 to 3 pounds boneless pork loin roast
1/3 cup olive oil
3 tablespoons lemon juice
1/2 teaspoon oregano, crushed
1/2 teaspoon rosemary
1/2 teaspoon thyme
4 whole cloves
8 peppercorns

Game Sauce
10-1/2 ounce can beef broth
1 quart boiling water
Peel of 1 orange, removed with vegetable peeler and julienned
2 tablespoons orange marmalade, preferably Seville
1 tablespoon red currant jelly
2 tablespoons chutney
2 tablespoons Worcestershire sauce
1 teaspoon catsup
2 tablespoons brandy

Whisk together the oil, lemon juice, herbs, cloves and peppercorns. Place the roast in a roasting pan and pour the marinade over. Turn the roast to coat well. Allow to stand at room temperature at least 1 hour or prepare early in day and refrigerate until ready to roast.

Preheat oven to 450 degrees. Spoon marinade over meat, place meat in oven and bake for 25 minutes. Reduce heat to 350 degrees and bake an additional 1-1/2 to 2 hours, depending on size of roast. Remove roast from pan, reserve juices. (Remove any strings from roast once it has cooled slightly.) Wrap in plastic wrap and refrigerate up to two days .

_____

_____

_____

Deglaze pan with beef broth, strain and refrigerate until fat rises to the surface and can be removed.

To make Game Sauce, drop julienned orange rind into boiling water and simmer about 5 minutes; drain, rinse with cold water and pat dry. Combine the orange rind, reserved juices from roast and remaining ingredients for sauce, except brandy, in a small saucepan and bring to a simmer over low heat. Pour brandy into a soup ladle and warm over the stove heat, ignite with a match and allow the alcohol to burn off; add to sauce and continue to simmer a few minutes. Taste for salt and pepper and adjust to taste. Cool and refrigerate. Sauce is best made a day before serving.

Prior to serving, slice meat slightly thinner than 1/2 inch thick. If serving hot, arrange in an ovenproof dish and spoon some sauce on top. Cover lightly with foil and heat 30 minutes in a preheated 325-degree oven. Heat sauce over low heat and serve separately in a sauceboat.

When serving cold, arrange on a serving platter, garnish with watercress or other greens and spoon a ribbon of sauce over center of meat slices. Pass remaining sauce in a sauceboat.

Serves 6.

Side Dishes

Side Dishes

So many of our main courses are complete in themselves, you may not need a side dish — except perhaps a fresh vegetable that has been washed and trimmed earlier and steamed at the last minute. However, if you're looking for a substantial vegetable or starch dish, this chapter has them.

Persian Rice

2 cups long grain white rice
3 cups chicken stock
1/2 cup pine nuts, toasted in butter
1/4 cup currants
6 dried apricots, finely chopped
2 cloves garlic, finely minced
1 bunch scallions, washed and cut into thin rounds, including some green
2 tablespoons olive oil
Salt and freshly ground black pepper to taste

Sauté onion and garlic in the olive oil until onion is translucent. Add the rice, stirring constantly, and sauté until most of the rice grains have turned milky. Add the nuts and fruit and salt and pepper. Blend.

About 30 minutes before serving, preheat oven to 375 degrees. Place rice mixture in a lidded casserole. Heat chicken stock to boiling, add to rice, stir, cover and place in oven for 20 to 25 minutes until stock is absorbed and rice is tender. Fluff with a fork and serve from casserole.

Serves 6.

Indian Rice

2 cups long grain rice (or basmati rice, washed and picked over)
3 cups chicken stock
2 cloves garlic, peeled and minced
2 canned hot chilis, seeded and chopped
1 teaspoon salt
1 teaspoon garam masala (available in Middle Eastern markets or specialty
   food stores)

Place all ingredients except chicken stock in an ovenproof, covered casserole. Set aside until 1/2 hour before serving. Preheat oven to 375 degrees; bring stock to a boil and pour over rice, stir briefly, cover and place in oven. Bake for 20 to 25 minutes until stock is absorbed and rice is tender. Fluff with a fork and serve from the casserole.

Serves 6.

Rice Pilaf Deluxe

1/3 cup butter or margarine
1-1/2 cups long grain rice
1 cup sliced mushrooms
1 cup chopped green onions
1 teaspoon oregano
1/2 teaspoon thyme
1/2 teaspoon marjoram
1 teaspoon salt
3 cups chicken broth
15-ounce can artichoke hearts, drained and halved
3/4 cup slivered almonds

Melt butter in large skillet, add rice, mushrooms and green onions. Sauté about 5 minutes. Add seasonings. Prepare early in day and set aside or refrigerate covered overnight. Transfer mixture to 2-quart casserole, stir in broth, artichokes and almonds.

Preheat oven to 325 degrees. Bake, covered, 1 hour. Uncover, fluff with fork. Baking time can be adjusted to higher oven temperature.

Serves 6.

Baked Brown Rice With Parsley

2 cups brown rice
1/4 cup butter, melted
3 cups boiling chicken or beef broth (flavor depends on the entree)
2 cloves garlic, minced, optional
1/3 cup chopped parsley
Salt to taste

Melt butter in medium-sized skillet. Add rice and stir until coated with butter. Transfer to a 1-1/2 quart casserole, set aside.

Thirty-five minutes before serving, add boiling broth and optional garlic to casserole. Cover tightly and bake in preheated 350-degree oven. Fluff rice with fork and stir in chopped parsley. Taste for salt and adjust as necessary.

Serves 6.

Bulgur Wheat and Chick Pea Pilaf

3 tablespoons olive oil
1/2 cup chopped onions
1/2 cup broken, uncooked vermicelli or thin spaghetti
1 cup bulgur wheat
2-1/2 cups chicken broth
1 teaspoon salt
1/4 teaspoon pepper
6 tablespoons chopped fresh basil or 2 tablespoons dried basil
1/4 cup coarsely chopped walnuts
3/4 cup canned chick peas, drained

Heat oil in large saucepan, add onions and sauté briefly. Add vermicelli and sauté until onions and pasta are golden, stirring constantly. Add bulgur wheat and sauté only a minute or two. Add remaining ingredients, bring to boil. Transfer to casserole, cover and set aside if using later in day, or cover and refrigerate if using following day. Bring to room temperature, stir with fork and bake, covered, in 325-degree oven for 30 minutes. Bake for shorter length of time if oven is at a higher temperature for another baked dish.

Serves 6.

Barley and Mushroom Casserole

1-1/2 cups pearl barley
1/4 cup butter or margarine
1/2 pound mushrooms, thickly sliced
4 tablespoons dry onion soup mix
2-1/2 cups chicken broth
1 cup sliced almonds
1 teaspoon marjoram or thyme
3 tablespoons dry sherry

In large saucepan, melt butter and brown barley. Add mushrooms, onion soup mix, broth, almonds and marjoram or thyme and sherry. Stir together, bring to boil, cover and simmer 10 minutes. Transfer to casserole, cover and set aside if using later in day, or cover and refrigerate up to 2 days.

Bring to room temperature, stir with fork and bake covered in 350-degree oven for 45 minutes. Stir once with fork.

Serves 6.

French Potato Salad

12 small new potatoes, about 2 pounds, scrubbed but not peeled
1/2 cup dry white vermouth
4 tablespoons olive oil
1 tablespoon vinegar
2 shallots, peeled and chopped (or 8-10 scallions, sliced)
1/2 cup minced parsley
Salt and freshly ground black pepper to taste

Simmer potatoes in water to cover until just tender, about 12 to 15 minutes. While potatoes are still warm, slice into rounds. Place in serving dish and add vermouth, turning potatoes so they can absorb the wine. Let sit about 15 minutes. Add rest of ingredients, mix well but gently so potatoes do not fall apart. Cover and refrigerate up to 24 hours. Before serving, taste for salt and pepper and adjust as necessary. Serve lightly chilled.

Serves 6.

Oven Parsley-Garlic Potatoes

3 pounds baking potatoes, peeled and sliced slightly thicker than potato chips
    in food processor or on hand grater
4 cloves garlic, peeled and minced
1/2 cup minced parsley
Salt and freshly ground black pepper to taste
1/4 to 1/2 cup olive oil

In an ovenproof serving dish, place potatoes and other ingredients, adjusting amount of olive oil so that potatoes are well coated but there is little extra oil in the dish. Mix well, cover with plastic wrap and refrigerate. (Any discoloration of potatoes disappears on cooking.)

Thirty minutes before serving, unwrap and place in a 400-degree oven; bake until potatoes are cooked through and crispy at the edges. For a browner top, place under broiler for 2 or 3 minutes.

Serves 6.

Potato and Fruit Gratin

5 cups sliced potatoes (1/4-inch thick slices)
6 tablespoons butter or margarine
1 tablespoon vegetable oil
2 Granny Smith or other tart apples, sliced but not peeled
2 medium onions, sliced
1-pound can apricots, drained and thickly sliced
3 cups chicken broth

In large skillet, melt 2 tablespoons butter and 1 tablespoon oil; add half of potatoes and fry until lightly browned. Remove to large shallow baking dish. Add more butter if needed and fry remaining potatoes. Add to dish. Sprinkle with salt. Melt 2 tablespoons butter, add apples and sauté briefly. Do not sauté until soft. Spread over potatoes in baking dish.

Melt 2 tablespoons butter, sauté onions until quite brown. Add to baking dish on top of apples. Sprinkle with salt.

Scatter sliced apricots over top of onions. Pour chicken broth into dish.

Cover with foil and refrigerate up to three days before serving.

Bring to room temperature, remove foil and bake 1 hour in 350-degree oven or until most of broth has been absorbed.

Serves 6.

Roast Potato Wedges With Herbs

6 baking potatoes
1/3 cup vegetable oil
1 tablespoon olive oil
2 teaspoons rosemary or 1 tablespoon fresh rosemary
2 teaspoons marjoram or 1 tablespoon fresh marjoram
2 teaspoons salt
1/4 teaspoon pepper

Mix seasonings and oil in a large bowl. Scrub potatoes, dry, cut into thick wedges (halve lengthwise, cut halves in thirds). Add to bowl, mix thoroughly to coat; cover bowl.

Preheat oven to 375 degrees. Spread potatoes in single layer on flat metal pan. Bake 45 minutes. Turn wedges once to brown evenly.

Serves 6.

Potatoes With Pizazz

3 tablespoons butter, divided
3 cloves garlic, minced
6 medium potatoes, peeled and thinly sliced
1 teaspoon rosemary
Salt and pepper
1-1/2 cups grated sharp Cheddar or Gruyere cheese
2-1/2 cups chicken broth
1/2 cup dry bread crumbs

Grease a 7 x 11 glass baking dish with small amount of butter. Sprinkle with minced garlic. Add layer of half of the potato slices, sprinkle with half the rosemary, salt and pepper and half the cheese.

Add remaining potatoes, making a flat layer on top. Sprinkle with rosemary, salt and pepper and remaining cheese. Dot with 1 tablespoon butter.

Pour broth into dish, not over potatoes and cheese.

Bake, covered, in preheated 350-degree oven for 1 hour. Cool to room temperature. Can be refrigerated up to 2 days before serving. Can also be frozen. Wrap in plastic wrap, then foil. Thaw overnight in refrigerator.

Bring to room temperature. Uncover, sprinkle with breadcrumbs and dot with 2 tablespoons butter.

Bake in 375-degree oven 30-40 minutes or until crumbs are lightly browned and potatoes soft.

Serves 6.

Family Favorite Potatoes

8 medium potatoes, peeled and sliced
2 medium onions, sliced
1/2 teaspoon thyme
Salt and pepper
1/4 cup chopped parsley
1/4 cup butter or margarine
1-1/2 cups beef broth

Arrange layer of potatoes and onions in bottom of buttered 7 x 11 inch glass baking dish. Sprinkle with thyme, salt and pepper. Repeat layer of potatoes, onions and seasonings. Scatter chopped parsley on top. Dot butter on top. Pour broth into dish, not over potatoes.

Bake, covered with foil, 30 minutes in preheated 350-degree oven. Cool, then refrigerate up to 2 days before serving.

Remove from refrigerator about 2 hours before serving. Bake, uncovered, in preheated 350-degree oven for 1 hour.

Serves 6.

Noodle Casserole

12 ounces broad egg noodles, cooked
2 10-ounce packages frozen chopped spinach (thawed and liquid squeezed out)
1/4 cup butter or margarine
1 large onion, chopped
3 eggs, lightly beaten
1 cup sour cream
1-1/2 teaspoons salt
1/4 teaspoon pepper
1/4 teaspoon nutmeg
1/2 teaspoon thyme

Mix noodles and spinach in large bowl. Melt butter in medium skillet, sauté onions until golden; add to noodles. Fold in eggs, sour cream and seasonings. Pour into well-buttered 2-quart casserole.

Cover and refrigerate up to 1 day before serving.

Remove from refrigerator about 2 hours before baking. Preheat oven to 350 degrees. Bake casserole, uncovered, 45 minutes.

Serves 6.

Grits and Cheese Bake

4 cups water
1 cup quick-cooking (not instant) grits
1 teaspoon salt
2 tablespoons butter or margarine
2 cups shredded sharp Cheddar cheese
2 cloves garlic, minced
2 eggs, well beaten
1/4 cup chopped pimento

Bring water to boil, add salt and stir in grits in a slow, steady stream.
Reduce heat to low; cook 5 minutes, stirring occasionally. Add butter,
cheese and garlic. Stir until cheese is almost melted. Remove from heat.
Add small amount of grits to beaten eggs; stir eggs into remaining grits.
Add chopped pimento. Pour mixture into well-buttered 2-quart casserole.
Cover and refrigerate up to 2 days.

Bring to room temperature before baking. Preheat oven to 350 degrees.
Bake, uncovered, 35-40 minutes.

Serves 6.

Corn Pudding

3 boxes frozen corn kernels
Butter
4 eggs
1-1/2 cups whole milk or half-and-half
1 teaspoon Worcestershire sauce
2-3 dashes hot pepper sauce
Salt and freshly ground black pepper to taste

Cook the frozen corn in lightly salted water until just done, about 2-3 minutes. Drain well, season generously with butter, salt and pepper. Let cool.

Beat the eggs until light, add the milk or cream and the two sauces. Stir in the corn. Taste for seasonings and adjust as necessary. Refrigerate until 1 hour before baking.

About 50 minutes before serving, preheat oven to 350 degrees. Pour corn mixture into a well-buttered ovenproof casserole or ring mold; set container in another pan containing hot but not boiling water. Bake about 40 minutes or until a knife inserted near the edge comes out clean. Let rest about 10 minutes before serving.

Serves 6.

Zucchini and Walnut Sauté

1-1/2 pounds zucchini, cut in 1/2 inch slices
1 tablespoon olive oil
2 tablespoons butter, divided
1 large garlic clove, minced
1/3 cup coarsely chopped walnuts
1/2 teaspoon salt or more to taste
1/4 teaspoon freshly ground black pepper

Early in day scrub zucchini and slice. Refrigerate in plastic, air-tight bag or in bowl tightly covered with plastic wrap.

Sauté walnuts in 1 tablespoon butter, set aside.

Shortly before serving first course or while preparing entree for the table, melt 1 tablespoon butter and oil together in large skillet over moderately high heat. Add zucchini slices and garlic, salt and pepper. Quickly brown. Turn zucchini, add walnuts and sauté 1 minute more. Transfer to serving bowl.

Serves 6.

Winter Squash With Fruit

3 pounds butternut or hubbard squash, peeled and cut in 2-inch cubes
1/2 cup fresh orange juice
2 tablespoons butter or margarine
2 tablespoons brown sugar
1/2 teaspoon salt
1 green apple, unpeeled, cut in 1-inch cubes
1 cup fresh cranberries
1/2 cup golden raisins

Early in day or day before serving put prepared squash in flat baking dish. Scatter apples, cranberries and raisins on top. Sprinkle with salt. Heat orange juice, butter and sugar to boiling, pour over squash and fruit.

Cover tightly with foil and refrigerate up to two hours before baking.

Preheat oven to 350 degrees. Bake squash, covered, 35 to 45 minutes depending on tenderness desired.

Serves 6.

Butternut Squash and Carrot Mock Soufflé

2 pounds butternut squash, peeled and diced
1 pound carrots, peeled and sliced
1 small onion, quartered
1 teaspoon salt
1/2 cup light cream
1/4 cup butter or margarine
1/2 teaspoon dried dillweed
1/8 teaspoon cayenne pepper
Salt to taste
Minced parsley for garnish

Add squash, carrots, onion and salt to boiling water. Cook until soft. Drain.

Transfer half of vegetables and half of cream and butter to bowl of food processor. Process until smooth, remove. Repeat with remaining vegetables, cream and butter. Mix in seasonings and taste for salt.

Transfer to buttered 1-quart casserole. Cover with plastic wrap and refrigerate up to 3 days before serving.

Remove casserole from refrigerator at least 2 hours before serving. Bake in preheated 350-degree oven for 30 minutes. Sprinkle with minced parsley before serving.

Serves 6.

Sue's Spinach Casserole

2 10-ounce boxes frozen spinach, cooked and drained
8-ounce package cream cheese, softened
1/2 cup butter or margarine, divided
1 teaspoon rosemary
1/2 teaspoon salt
1/4 teaspoon freshly ground pepper
1 cup herbed bread cubes

Mix spinach with cream cheese, 1/4 cup butter, rosemary, salt and pepper. Spoon spinach mixture into well-buttered 1-1/2-quart casserole dish. Melt 1/4 cup butter, toss with bread cubes. Scatter on top of spinach mixture. Cover with plastic wrap and refrigerate up to 2 days before serving.

Remove casserole from refrigerator at least 2 hours before baking. Preheat oven to 350 degrees. Bake spinach casserole, uncovered, 30 minutes.

Serves 6.

Mushrooms Au Gratin

1-1/2 pounds mushrooms, thickly sliced
1 cup grated Cheddar cheese
1 cup black olives, sliced
2 tablespoons flour
1 teaspoon salt
1/4 teaspoon pepper
1/2 cup half and half or light cream
2 tablespoons butter or margarine
1-1/2 cup fresh breadcrumbs

In a 1-1/2-quart buttered casserole layer half of mushrooms, cheese and olives. Repeat layer with remaining mushrooms, cheese and olives.

Mix together flour, salt, pepper and half and half. Pour over mushrooms.

In a small saucepan melt butter, add bread crumbs and toss. Sprinkle over mushrooms. Cover with plastic wrap and refrigerate overnight or prepare early in day before baking.

Remove casserole from refrigerator 1 hour before baking. Preheat oven to 350 degrees. Bake, uncovered, 30 minutes.

Serves 6.

Creamed Bermuda Onions

5 large Bermuda onions, peeled and thickly sliced
1/4 cup butter or margarine
1/2 teaspoon salt and freshly ground pepper to taste
1 teaspoon marjoram
1 teaspoon sugar
1/2 cup heavy cream
1/4 cup chopped green onion tops

Melt butter in large skillet, stir in onion slices. Cover and cook over low heat about 25 minutes. Remove cover, add salt, pepper, marjoram and sugar. Continue to cook over high heat, stirring occasionally, until onions are golden.

Remove from heat, stir in cream. Return to heat and cook until cream has thickened slightly. Spoon into bowl, cover with plastic wrap and refrigerate up to three days before serving.

Remove from refrigerator, stir in chopped green onion tops and reheat over low heat in medium skillet. Or transfer to 1-quart baking dish and reheat in oven for 20-25 minutes with other food that is baking.

Serves 6.

Baked Sweet Carrots

12 medium carrots, approximately the same size, peeled and trimmed
2 cups chicken broth
3 tablespoons brown sugar
1/2 teaspoon salt
1/4 cup butter
Lemon slices and parsley for garnish, optional

Simmer whole carrots in the chicken broth until just tender, about 15 minutes. Drain (reserve stock for soup). In a flameproof casserole with a cover, melt butter with the brown sugar and salt. Add carrots, turning to coat well; cool, cover and refrigerate.

Thirty minutes before serving, preheat oven to 375 degrees. Heat carrots and butter mixture over very low heat on top of stove until butter sizzles. Cover casserole and heat in oven until very hot. Place carrots on a white oval platter and pour the butter sauce over. Garnish platter with thin lemon slices and parsley if desired.

Serves 6.

Baked Carrots Delicious

1 pound carrots, plus 3 carrots
1/2 teaspoon salt
1/4 teaspoon pepper
1 teaspoon sugar
2 tablespoons horseradish
1/2 cup mayonnaise
3/4 cup dry breadcrumbs

Wash and peel carrots; cut crosswise in thirds, then lengthwise into strips. Cook about 10 minutes in boiling salted water. Drain. Transfer carrots to buttered 1-quart casserole. Sprinkle with salt, pepper and sugar.

Mix horseradish and mayonnaise in small bowl. Spread over carrots. Sprinkle crumbs over top. Cover with plastic wrap and refrigerate up to 2 days before serving.

Remove casserole from refrigerator at least 2 hours before baking. Preheat oven to 350 degrees. Bake carrots, uncovered, 20-25 minutes.

Serves 6.

Carrot and Apple Casserole

8 medium carrots, cut in half-inch rounds
6 Golden Delicious apples, peeled and sliced
1/3 cup honey
1 teaspoon freshly grated ginger or 1/2 teaspoon powdered ginger
1/2 teaspoon salt
2 tablespoons butter

Add carrot slices to boiling, salted water; cook 10-15 minutes, or until barely tender. Drain.

Toss carrots with apples, honey, ginger and salt. Transfer to a shallow, buttered baking dish; dot with butter. Cover with foil. Bake in preheated 350- degree oven 20 minutes. Cool, then refrigerate up to 3 days before serving.

Remove from refrigerator up to 2 hours before reheating. Preheat oven to 350 degrees, bake covered, 20 minutes; remove foil, stir and bake uncovered 10 minutes.

Serves 6.

Apple and Onion Casserole

6 Granny Smith or other tart apples, cored and sliced
3 large yellow onions, sliced
1/2 cup brown sugar
1/4 cup butter or margarine, melted
1 teaspoon salt
1/4 teaspoon freshly ground pepper or more to taste
1-1/2 tablespoons butter or margarine
1/3 cup breadcrumbs

Butter a 1-1/2-quart casserole. Arrange half of onions in bottom; cover with 1/4 cup brown sugar and season with half the salt and pepper. Dot with half the butter.

Arrange apples on top; cover with remaining onions, brown sugar, seasonings and dot with butter.

Mix breadcrumbs with melted butter; sprinkle on top. Bake in preheated 300-degree oven 1 hour. Cover with foil and refrigerate up to 3 days before serving.

Remove from refrigerator about 2 hours before baking. Bake uncovered in preheated 350-degree oven for 20 minutes.

Serves 6.

Ratatouille

1 firm, unblemished eggplant, about 1 pound, washed and cut into 1-inch
   cubes
3 small zucchini, washed, trimmed and sliced
1 large onion, peeled and sliced
2 green peppers, seeded and cut into long strips
2 cloves garlic, minced
1 bay leaf
1/4 teaspoon leaf thyme
16-ounce can Italian plum tomatoes, roughly chopped, with their juice
4 tablespoons olive oil
Salt and freshly ground black pepper to taste

In a large flameproof casserole, sauté eggplant in batches in the olive oil until lightly browned. Add rest of ingredients to eggplant and oil; bring to a boil, reduce heat and simmer vegetables uncovered for 30 to 45 minutes, until liquid thickens and vegetables are cooked but still distinguishable. Cool, cover and refrigerate at least 24 hours to allow flavors to blend. Before serving, taste for salt and pepper and adjust as necessary; remove bay leaf. May be served cold or reheated.

Can be prepared up to 1 week before serving.

Serves 6.

Vegetables Vinaigrette: A Compendium

A cold or room temperature dish of vegetables, cooked or raw, dressed in a vinaigrette can serve as both the side dish and the salad. Below are some suggested combinations. To prepare, simply blend dressing ingredients and pour over vegetables, cover and refrigerate up to 24 hours in advance. Stir gently from time to time. Taste for seasonings before serving and adjust as necessary. Serves 6.

#1

1 box cherry tomatoes, washed and stemmed
1 can hearts of palm, drained and sliced into 1-inch pieces on the diagonal
1 green and 1 yellow (or red) sweet pepper, seeded and cut into squares
3 tablespoons olive oil
2 tablespoons red wine vinegar or balsamic vinegar
Salt and freshly ground black pepper to taste

#2

1/2 box cherry tomatoes, washed and stemmed
1 small zucchini, washed, trimmed and cut into thin rounds
1 small yellow squash, washed, trimmed and cut into thin rounds
1 cucumber, peeled, halved lengthwise, seeded and cut into half rounds
1 green pepper, washed, seeded and cut into squares
1 cup broccoli or cauliflower florets, washed and drained
4 tablespoons olive oil
2 tablespoons red wine vinegar
1 teaspoon dried dillweed
Salt and freshly ground black pepper to taste

#3

1-1/2 pounds green or round beans, trimmed, washed and steamed until just
    crisp-tender
1 red pepper, seeded and cut into matchsticks
1 medium red onion, peeled, cut in half and thinly sliced
3 tablespoons olive oil
2 tablespoons red wine vinegar
1 teaspoon Dijon-style mustard
Salt and freshly ground black pepper to taste

#4

36 thin stalks asparagus, washed and trimmed, then steamed until just tender
3 tablespoons vegetable oil
1 teaspoon sesame oil
1 tablespoon soy sauce
1 tablespoon red wine vinegar
2 tablespoons sesame seeds
Salt and freshly ground black pepper to taste

#5

1 pound snowpeas, blanched for 1 minute in boiling water
1/2 cup chopped walnuts
1 red pepper, seeded and cut into matchsticks
1 tablespoon vegetable oil
1 tablespoon soy sauce
1 teaspoon sesame oil
2 drops hot Chinese oil
Salt and freshly ground black pepper to taste

#6

24 fat stalks asparagus, trimmed and steamed until just tender
3 tablespoons olive oil
Juice of one lemon
Salt and freshly ground black pepper to taste

#7

3 cucumbers, peeled, halved lengthwise, seeded and sliced into half-rounds
2 tablespoons olive oil
2 tablespoons balsamic vinegar (or red wine vinegar and 1/2 teaspoon sugar)
1 teaspoon dried dillweed or 2 tablespoons fresh snipped dill
Salt and freshly ground black pepper to taste

#8

2 boxes frozen corn kernels, cooked and drained
1 red pepper, seeded and cut in a small dice
1 bunch scallions, washed and sliced into rounds, including some green
3 tablespoons salad oil
2 tablespoons red wine vinegar
1 teaspoon dried dillweed or 2 tablespoons fresh snipped dill
Salt and freshly ground black pepper to taste

Marinated Mixed Vegetables

1/2 cup extra-virgin olive oil
1/4 cup white wine vinegar
1 tablespoon Dijon mustard
1 teaspoon salt
1/2 teaspoon freshly ground pepper
1/2 teaspoon sugar
1 teaspoon tarragon, crushed
1/2 teaspoon basil, crushed
2 large broccoli spears, tops broken into small florets and top 2 inches of
    stalk peeled and sliced
1/2 head cauliflower, cut into small pieces
1/4 pound green beans, cut into 1-inch pieces
1 large stalk celery, cut diagonally into thin slices
1 large sweet red pepper, seeded and cut into 1-inch squares
1 yellow squash, halved lengthwise then sliced across
12 small cherry tomatoes
4 green onions, sliced diagonally into 1/2-inch pieces

Combine oil, vinegar, mustard and seasonings in a small bowl and whisk together.

Add all vegetables to a glass bowl or plastic container. Pour dressing over and mix gently. Cover and marinate in refrigerator overnight. Stir occasionally.

Serves 6.

Italian Toast

1 loaf best Italian bread, sliced in 3/4-inch thick slices
6 tablespoons olive oil
3 tablespoons red wine vinegar
2 cloves garlic, peeled and put through a garlic press
Salt and freshly ground black pepper to taste
1/2 teaspoon red pepper flakes

Place bread slices on a cookie sheet. Whisk together other ingredients, spread generously on the bread. Cover with plastic wrap and refrigerate. About 10 minutes before serving, unwrap and place in a 400-degree oven. Bake until hot and crispy. Serve in a breadbasket lined with a cloth napkin.

Serves 6.

Desserts

Desserts

*W*ith so many dieters around these days, you might want to warn your guests to "save room" if you've planned something spectacular. On the other hand, a simple fruit dessert often satisfies everyone, so we've included numerous recipes for those. If time is short, the "gourmet" ice creams and sorbets now in supermarkets are more than satisfactory. Check out the local farmers' market or specialty food shops for ready-made desserts with a homemade flavor.

Fresh Fruit Compendium

*T*oday's lighter meals and more balanced menus mean a fresh fruit dessert is often a perfect ending. To add a bit of crunch to fruit desserts, try our Dreamy Short Cookies, Oatmeal Lace Cookies, Lucille's Shortbread, your own plain favorite or cookies from the neighborhood bakery.

Poached Pears
With Raspberry Vinegar

6 pears, ripe but firm
3 cups water
1 cup sugar
4 tablespoons raspberry vinegar
3 whole cloves

Combine water and sugar in deep saucepan and cook until sugar dissolves. Add vinegar and cloves; simmer for 10 minutes. Peel pears, leaving on stem, and add to syrup. Simmer about 20 minutes, turning several times. Do not overcook.

Transfer pears and syrup to an attractive serving dish; cool. Cover with plastic wrap and refrigerate up to 3 days before serving. Serve pears cold with a little syrup.

Serves 6.

Peachy Mustard Pears

6 pears, ripe but firm
1 cup peach preserves
4 tablespoons Dijon mustard
1/2 cup water
2 tablespoons apple juice
2 tablespoons lemon juice
2 2-inch strips lemon peel

Peel, quarter and core pears. In a large skillet, mix together peach preserves, Dijon mustard, water, apple juice, lemon juice and lemon peel. Add pear quarters and coat with mixture. Cover, cook gently over very low heat about 10 minutes or until pears are slightly soft.

Transfer to serving bowl, cool. Cover with plastic wrap and refrigerate up to three days before serving. Serve at room temperature.

Serves 6.

Fresh Fruit Compote

Select three of the suggested fruits. Adjust amounts given based on the fruits used.

2 large apples, cored and diced
1 box blueberries, rinsed and picked over
1 ripe cantaloupe or other melon, rind removed and diced
2 cups pineapple chunks, fresh or canned in juice
1 pint strawberries, washed, hulled and sliced
3 navel oranges, segmented and white pith removed
2 firm bananas, diced (add shortly before serving)
3 kiwi fruits, peeled and sliced into rounds
1 large very ripe mango or papaya, peeled, seeded and diced
1/2 pound sweet Bing or other red cherries
3 tablespoons orange liqueur, kirsch or creme de cassis
Brown sugar to taste, about 2 tablespoons
1/4 teaspoon cinnamon
1/2 cup orange juice

Combine the three selected fruits in a large glass serving bowl. Add liqueur of choice, sugar, orange juice and cinnamon; mix gently. Cover with plastic wrap, refrigerate overnight or at least 1 hour to let fruits macerate.

Serves 6.

Strawberries and Mozzarella

1 quart fresh strawberries
3 ounces whole-milk mozzarella, preferably buffalo-milk mozzarella
1 tablespoon raspberry vinegar
1 tablespoon water
3 tablespoons sugar
Freshly ground black pepper
Mint leaves or lemon basil leaves for garnish

Rinse and hull berries, halve if large; set aside. Cube mozzarella into 1/2-inch dice, add to berries; do not mix.

Dissolve sugar in vinegar and water. Pour over strawberries and cheese, mix gently with rubber spatula or wooden spoon. Cover with plastic wrap, refrigerate overnight. Before serving, mix gently again. Grind a generous amount of black pepper on top. Transfer to attractive serving bowl, garnish with mint or lemon-basil leaves. For a bit of "at-table drama," grind the pepper onto the fruit just before serving.

Serves 6.

Berries in Berry Sauce

1 pint strawberries, rinsed, hulled and halved
1 pint blueberries, rinsed and picked over
1 box frozen raspberries, thawed, drained and puréed
2 tablespoons kirsch or crème de cassis
Vanilla ice cream, softened, optional

Put strawberries and blueberries into serving dish, preferably clear glass. Cover with plastic, refrigerate overnight.

Mix puréed raspberries with liqueur of your choice, refrigerate overnight.

Just before serving, add raspberry sauce to berries, mix gently. Serve over vanilla ice cream, if desired.

Serves 6.

Peaches in Spiced Chardonnay

6-8 fresh peaches or 2 16-ounce cans natural-juice-packed freestone peach halves, drained
1 cup chardonnay
1/4 cup water
1 cup sugar
2 3-inch cinnamon sticks
6 whole cloves
6 whole allspice berries, lightly crushed
1/2-inch slice fresh ginger root, lightly crushed
Juice of 1/2 lemon

In a stainless steel pan, mix wine, water, sugar, cinnamon sticks, cloves, allspice berries and ginger root. Cover, cook over low heat until sugar dissolves. Uncover, raise heat to high and boil until lightly syrupy, about 10 minutes. Cool to room temperature, discard ginger root.

Wash but do not peel fresh peaches; quarter either fresh or tinned peaches; place in attractive serving bowl. Mix gently with lemon juice. Pour wine syrup over peaches and mix gently. (A rubber spatula is best for mixing fresh fruit.) Cover with plastic wrap, refrigerate up to 2 days before serving. Serve at room temperature or lightly chilled.

Serves 6.

Gingered Melon

4 cups honeydew melon, cantaloupe or other firm melon, or combination of melons
1-1/2 cups water
3/4 cup sugar
1 tablespoon finely chopped fresh ginger root
Seeds of 4 cardamom pods
Crushed Italian macaroons (amaretti), if available

In a small stainless steel pan, mix water, sugar, ginger root and cardamom seeds. Bring to a boil, reduce heat and simmer 15 minutes. Cool thoroughly.

Cut melon in half, remove seeds. Cut in wedges and remove fruit from rind, then cube or use melon ball tool to scoop from rind. (A combination of cubes and balls is nice.) Strain the ginger and cardamom seeds from the syrup and pour syrup over melon.

Cover with plastic wrap and refrigerate overnight. Serve lightly chilled, garnished with crushed macaroons.

Serves 6.

Figs Poached in Red Wine

Something a little different to serve at the end of a Middle Eastern meal. Look for dried figs packaged in a ring and held together with string—they have more substance than the boxed California variety.

24 dried figs (see above note)
2 cups dry red wine
3/4 cup sugar
1 tablespoon lemon juice
Zest from 1 lemon
1 bay leaf
3 peppercorns
1 cinnamon stick, or 1/4 teaspoon powdered cinnamon

In a non-aluminum pan, bring all ingredients except the figs to a boil, then simmer about 10 minutes. Add figs and simmer another 10 minutes, or until figs are soft but not mushy. Let figs cool in the poaching liquid, then cover pan and refrigerate for up to 24 hours.

Remove figs from poaching liquid before serving. Serve plain or with Custard Sauce.

Serves 6.

Custom Sauce

*Custard sauce, crème Anglaise or simple boiled custard. Whatever its
name, this childhood confection has myriad uses—with any poached fruit,
fresh fruit, baked fruit crisps and compotes, or with puddings and ice
cream. Be sure to cook the custard over a very low heat and stir constantly
or it may curdle. If that does happen, you can sometimes save at least part
of it by straining out the solid particles and whirling the rest in the blender.*

7 egg yolks
3 cups milk
1/2 cup sugar
2 teaspoons vanilla or 2 tablespoons fruit brandy such as Grand Marnier

Scald the milk (bring almost to a boil). While milk is heating, whisk
together egg yolks and sugar in a heavy pan. Gradually add the scalded
milk, whisking the entire time. Place the pan over very low heat and
continue whisking the mixture until it thickens—it will coat the whisk or
a tablespoon. Do not let mixture boil or it will curdle. Stir in the vanilla or
brandy. Cool, cover and refrigerate for up to 3 days.

Makes about 3-1/2 cups.

Baked Fruit Compote

This canned compote is the perfect answer when a fruit dessert is called for but the supermarkets are "between seasons" and offering only uninspiring and expensive fresh fruits. Serve hot in cold weather with Custard Sauce, or in warmer weather, chilled with vanilla ice cream.

16-ounce can apricot halves, drained
16-ounce can pear halves, drained
16-ounce can freestone peach halves, drained
16-ounce can pitted plums, drained
1/2 cup orange juice
3 tablespoons cassis (currant liqueur)
2 tablespoons brown sugar

Arrange drained fruits in an open casserole, sprinkle with the orange juice, cassis and sugar. Bake, uncovered in a 350-degree oven, for 20 to 30 minutes until bubbly and syrup has thickened slightly. Baste at least once during baking. Cool, cover and refrigerate.

If you wish to serve the compote hot, place casserole in a 300-degree oven just before sitting down to dinner.

Serves 6.

Peach or Apple and Blueberry Crisp

*F*resh *juicy peaches or crisp baking apples, blueberries and a quick batter can be baked together the night before the party. Top with vanilla ice cream or Custard Sauce.*

6 fresh peaches or 5 medium apples
1 cup blueberries
1-1/2 cups unsifted flour
3/4 cup brown sugar
2 teaspoons baking powder
1/2 teaspoon salt
1 teaspoon cinnamon
1 egg, beaten with 2 tablespoons water
1/2 cup melted butter

Butter 8-inch glass baking dish. Preheat oven to 350 degrees.

Wash peaches or apples; do not peel. Remove stones from peaches or core apples. Slice 1/4-inch thick. Mix with blueberries and put into baking dish. Mix dry ingredients with fork, stir in egg beaten with water. Spread over top of fruit. Pour melted butter over top. Bake 40 minutes. Remove to cake rack and cool thoroughly. Cover with plastic wrap, refrigerate.

Bring to room temperature, reheat in 325-degree oven 15 minutes before sitting down to dinner.

Serves 6.

Butter Crust Apple Kuchen

*H*ere *is an easier but no less tasty version of a long-time favorite. You might like to serve coffee with a hint of orange flavor to enhance the orange peel in the crust.*

2 cups unsifted flour
3 tablespoons sugar
2 teaspoons grated orange peel
1/2 teaspoon baking powder
1/4 teaspoon salt
1/2 cup butter, cut into 8 slices

4 tart apples, such as Granny Smith
1/2 cup sugar
1 teaspoon cinnamon
2 egg yolks, lightly beaten
1 cup heavy cream
1 teaspoon vanilla

Preheat oven to 400 degrees.

Mix together flour, sugar, baking powder, salt and orange peel. Cut in pieces of butter until crumbly. If available, use food processor fitted with steel blade. Pat mixture firmly onto bottom and partially up sides of an 8-inch glass baking dish.

Wash, core but do not peel apples. Slice into approximately 1/4-inch thick wedges. If available, use wide slicer of food processor. Arrange in neat rows over crumb crust. Combine 1/2 cup sugar and cinnamon; sprinkle over apples. Bake 15 minutes.

Mix together egg yolks, cream and vanilla; pour over apples. Return to oven, bake 30 minutes longer.

Cool completely on cake rack. Cover with plastic wrap and refrigerate up to 2 days. Can also be frozen; wrap foil tightly over plastic wrap. Thaw in refrigerator after removing foil wrap. Discard plastic wrap before reheating.

Place in 300-degree oven for 15 minutes before sitting down to dinner so kuchen will be warm at serving time.

Serves 6.

Apple Crisp

Perfect fall dessert.

6 Golden Delicious apples (or other cooking apples)
2 tablespoons water
1/4 cup sugar
1-1/2 cups prepared biscuit mix
1/2 cup sugar
1/2 teaspoon cinnamon
1 egg
1/4 cup solid vegetable shortening

Preheat oven to 400 degrees. Grease 8-inch-square glass baking dish.

Peel and slice apples thin; arrange in pan and sprinkle with the water and 1/4 cup of sugar.

In a bowl, stir together biscuit mix, 1/2 cup sugar, and the cinnamon. Beat egg separately and slowly pour into biscuit mixture, stirring with a fork until crumbly. Sprinkle mixture evenly over apples.

In a small pan, heat shortening until melted. Pour carefully over the biscuit mixture.

Bake apple crisp until browned, about 25 minutes. Cool. Wrap with plastic wrap and refrigerate overnight. Or wrap foil over plastic wrap and freeze. Serve warm, by reheating for 20 minutes in a 325-degree oven, or cold with the Custard Sauce or vanilla ice cream.

Serves 6.

Nellie's Berry Cobbler

A tasty way to celebrate berry season, whether you have done the picking yourself or visited your favorite fruit stand. Serve warm or chilled, as is or with vanilla ice cream.

4 cups berries, picked over and washed
1 cup sugar
1 teaspoon baking powder
Dash of salt
1 cup flour
3 tablespoons solid vegetable shortening
3/4 cup milk
1/2 cup sugar mixed with 1 tablespoon cornstarch
2/3 cup boiling water

Preheat oven to 375 degrees. Spread berries in bottom of greased deep baking dish.

In a bowl, mix together 1 cup of sugar, the baking powder, salt and flour. Cut in the shortening until mixture is crumbly. Stir in milk and pour mixture on top of berries. Sprinkle the 1/2 cup of sugar and cornstarch mixture on top. Pour the boiling water over all. (The batter will be thin.)

Bake for approximately 40 minutes until topping is quite brown. If not serving soon, cover and refrigerate or wrap well and freeze. May be reheated in a 325-degree oven for 20 minutes.

Serves 6.

Cold Orange Soufflé

This dessert is a refreshing and special ending to almost any of our entrees. You might like to pass a plate of Dreamy Short Cookies to nibble with the soufflé.

1 envelope unflavored gelatin
1/4 cup cold water
3 eggs, separated
1/2 cup sugar
2 tablespoons grated orange peel
2/3 cup fresh orange juice
1 teaspoon orange extract
1 cup heavy cream, whipped

Sprinkle gelatin over water in small saucepan, let stand to soften. Place pan over very low heat, stir until gelatin dissolves and mixture is clear. Remove from heat and cool.

Beat egg yolks until light in a large bowl. Gradually add sugar and beat until mixture is pale yellow and thick. Mix in orange peel, juice and orange extract. Add cooled gelatin mixture. Chill in refrigerator until mixture thickens slightly; stir occasionally.

Meanwhile, beat egg whites until stiff peaks form; set aside. In chilled bowl, beat cream until stiff. Refrigerate until orange mixture has thickened.

Fold egg whites and whipped cream into orange mixture. Spoon into 1-quart soufflé dish or other attractive dish with straight sides. Cover with plastic wrap and refrigerate 2 to 3 days before serving. Can be frozen; transfer to refrigerator early in day before serving.

Serves 6.

Quick Berry Mousse
With Peach Sauce

Cool and quick to make. You can vary the sauce with a splash of liqueur or try a variety of flavors for either mousse or sauce.

Mousse
1 10-ounce box frozen strawberries or raspberries
1 cup whipping cream
1 teaspoon lemon juice

Sauce
1 10-ounce box frozen peaches, thawed
1 tablespoon sugar
1 tablespoon peach brandy, cointreau, creme de cassis or liqueur of your
   choice (optional)

Put frozen strawberries or raspberries, whipping cream and lemon juice into food processor or blender. Blend until smooth and slightly thickened. Pour into 6 goblets or dessert dishes. Cover with plastic wrap and freeze. Remove from freezer just before sitting down to dinner. (If serving on a warm evening, place in refrigerator until serving time.)

Sauce: Place all ingredients in food processor or blender and blend until not quite smooth. Pour into serving bowl, cover with plastic wrap and refrigerate until serving time. Spoon over mousse or pass separately.

Serves 6.

Low-Calorie Lemon Mousse

Here is just the dessert for those observing diets or dietary restrictions. It's also the perfect ending to a hearty dinner. Add sliced oranges or peaches or bright berries for extra taste and color.

2 envelopes unflavored gelatin
3 tablespoons sugar or equivalent amount of sugar substitute
1-1/2 cups boiling water
3/4 cup fresh lemon juice (from 4-5 lemons)
2 teaspoons grated lemon peel
3 egg whites
3 tablespoons sugar or equal amount sugar substitute

In a large mixing bowl, mix gelatin and 3 tablespoons sugar; add boiling water; stir until dissolved. Add lemon juice and grated peel. Refrigerate about 2 hours or until slightly thickened.

In a small mixing bowl, beat egg whites until soft peaks form; gradually beat in remaining 3 tablespoons sugar. Beat until stiff peaks form.

Gently fold egg whites into slightly thickened lemon mixture. Pour into individual glass bowls or goblets. Cover each with plastic wrap. Refrigerate up to 3 days before serving.

Serves 6.

Frozen Lemon Crunch Torte With Raspberry Sauce

This dessert is a great finish to a hearty dinner of Moroccan Lamb Stew or Ossobucco; it's both sweet and tangy, smooth and textured—and surprisingly light.

12 Pepperidge Farm Lemon Crunch cookies, finely crushed
2 tablespoons finely chopped almonds
3 tablespoons melted butter
3 eggs, separated
2/3 cup sugar
1 cup heavy cream, whipped
1 tablespoon lemon rind
1/3 cup lemon juice
1 carton frozen raspberries, thawed and drained

Mix cookies, almonds and butter together and press into bottom of buttered 8-inch springform pan. Set aside.

Beat egg whites in large bowl. Gradually add sugar and beat until stiff peaks form. Beat egg yolks in small bowl until light yellow and thick. Add lemon rind and lemon juice. Beat cream in chilled bowl until stiff. Fold egg yolk mixture and cream into egg whites. Spoon mixture into springform pan. Freeze for several days or up to 2 weeks.

Prepare raspberries up to 2 days before serving. Thaw, drain and purée in blender or food processor, pour into attractive bowl, cover with plastic wrap and refrigerate.

Remove torte from freezer, discard plastic and foil wrap and place in refrigerator before sitting down to dinner. Do not remove sides of pan until ready to serve. Place torte on cake plate, cut and serve at the table. Spoon sauce around slices or pass separately.

Serves 6.

Lemon-Chocolate Charlotte

Where is it written that dessert can't consist entirely of off-the-shelf products, so long as it tastes great? If you don't have a springform pan, you can make "sandwiches" on individual dessert plates: Open three attached ladyfingers, spread bottom part with a half cup sherbet, cover with the top part, then coat with the chocolate sauce and freeze.

1 8-inch springform pan
Butter
2 packages plain ladyfingers, approximately
1 quart best quality lemon sherbet, approximately
8 ounces semisweet chocolate
4 tablespoons light cream or half and half

Butter sides of springform pan. Line with ladyfinger halves, browned side against rim of pan. (Trim ladyfingers so the rounded end just reaches the top of the pan.) Soften the sherbet so it is spreadable, and spread in pan to within 1 inch of top. Press sherbet firmly against ladyfingers. Put in freezer.

In the top half of a double boiler, melt the chocolate over, not in, simmering water. Stir in the cream. Let sauce cool a bit. Remove pan from freezer, pour sauce over top, spreading with a knife. Cover with plastic wrap and return to freezer. Allow sherbet to freeze firmly.

At serving time, remove sides from pan, place the charlotte on a footed cake plate. At the table, slice into wedges with a long sharp knife and serve on individual dessert plates.

Serves 6.

Layered Mocha Ice Cream Pie

Vary the ice cream flavors to your taste, but either your way or our way, this pie will keep in your freezer for weeks.

1 stick pie crust mix
1/4 cup sugar
1 teaspoon vanilla
2 tablespoons hot water
3/4 cup chopped pecans or walnuts
1 pint coffee ice cream, slightly softened
1 pint chocolate ice cream, slightly softened
1 cup whipping cream
2 tablespoons powdered sugar
1 tablespoon instant coffee (eliminate for fruit-flavored ice creams)

In a small bowl combine pie crust mix, vanilla, water and nuts, stir with a fork. Pat into 9-inch glass pie plate. Bake as directed on package.

Spoon coffee ice cream onto crust and smooth flat. Spoon chocolate ice cream carefully onto coffee layer, smooth flat. Place in freezer while preparing whipping cream.

In a small bowl dissolve instant coffee in cream. Partially whip before adding powdered sugar. Whip until stiff. Spread over ice cream pie.

Wrap entire pie in plastic wrap, then in foil. Freeze. Remove from freezer 1 hour before serving. Remove foil and place pie in refrigerator until serving time.

Serves 6.

Crème Caramel With Fresh Fruit

A rich baked custard, unmolded and the center filled with fresh berries sprinkled with kirsch, is a spectacular way to end a special dinner!

3/4 cup sugar

1 quart whole milk (or 2 cups milk and 2 cups half and half)

6 eggs

1/2 cup sugar

2 teaspoons vanilla

Dash of cinnamon

1 box blueberries, or other small berry, washed and picked over

3 tablespoons sugar

2 tablespoons kirsch

Prepare a 6-cup ring mold: In a small heavy skillet, preferably cast iron, melt sugar over very low heat until it turns a light tan. Carefully pour the very hot melted sugar into the ring mold; using potholders, swirl the ring mold so the sugar syrup covers the bottom. Set aside.

Preheat oven to 325 degrees. Heat about 1 quart of water.

To make custard, beat together the eggs, then add the milk, sugar, vanilla and cinnamon, stirring until sugar is dissolved. Pour the custard into the prepared ring mold, place mold in a larger baking pan, and pour the hot water into the pan until it reaches about halfway up the outside of the mold. Place pan in oven and bake custard for one hour or more, or until a knife inserted near the edge comes out clean. Remove mold from water and let cool. Cover with plastic wrap and refrigerate at least overnight.

Place berries, sugar and kirsch in a bowl, stir gently; cover and refrigerate, stirring from time to time.

On the day of the party, unmold custard by running a sharp knife around both edges of the ring mold, covering with the serving dish and inverting, tapping mold to dislodge custard if necessary. Pour the caramelized sugar syrup over the custard. Pile the fruit in the center.

Serves 6.

Lemony Bread Pudding

Old-fashioned lemony bread pudding makes a soothing ending to a simple meal. Especially good with Custard Sauce.

Pudding
12 slices good white bread, crusts trimmed and bread cut into a 1-inch dice
3 cups milk
4 egg yolks
Zest and juice of 1 lemon
1 teaspoon vanilla
1/4 cup currants
5 tablespoons sugar

Meringue Topping
4 egg whites
4 tablespoons powdered sugar

Preheat oven to 325 degrees. Heat about 1 quart of water until hot but not boiling.

Place the diced bread in a 2-quart open baking dish. Pour the milk over and let bread soak for 10-15 minutes. Meanwhile, whisk together egg yolks, lemon zest and juice, vanilla, and sugar until well blended. Add currants. Pour over the soaked bread and stir gently to mix. Place baking dish in another pan and pour one inch hot water in outer pan. Bake for 45 minutes to 1 hour until pudding begins to set. Cool.

To make meringue, beat egg whites with an electric mixer until smooth and glossy. Add powdered sugar a little at a time and continue beating egg whites until stiff but not dry. Spread or spoon over cooled pudding and bake in 350-degree oven until meringue is browned, about 15 minutes. Cool, cover with plastic wrap and refrigerate.

Serve with Custard Sauce or puréed frozen raspberries, if desired.

Serves 6.

Chocolate Chocolate Cake

This single layer chocolate cake is so moist and rich, it's almost like a dense pudding, yet it's very easy to whip together.

3/4 cup semisweet chocolate bits
1-1/2 cups flour
1/2 teaspoon salt
3-1/2 tablespoons cocoa
1 cup sugar
1 teaspoon baking powder
1 teaspoon vanilla
5 tablespoons vegetable oil
1 cup water
Whipped cream, optional

Preheat oven to 350 degrees. Grease 8-inch round cake pan. Place round of wax paper in bottom of pan, grease paper. Sprinkle with the chocolate bits.

In a mixing bowl, stir together dry ingredients. Whisk in the liquid ingredients until blended into a smooth batter. Pour over chocolate bits. Bake about 35 minutes, or until center of cake springs back to the touch. Cool in pan.

Cover with plastic wrap and refrigerate until cold. Run a knife around edge of pan, cover with a cake plate and invert. Slowly peel wax paper off.

Cake can also be frozen: remove from pan; wrap in plastic wrap and foil. Thaw unwrapped.

Slice into 6 or more wedges and serve with whipped cream if desired.

Serves 6.

Devil's Food Cake
Marie Larkin Connors

A childhood memory passed on by a good friend. A natural for birthdays, iced with your favorite frosting. Or make a one-layer version in a 9 x 13 inch pan and serve it with fudge or raspberry sauce.

2 cups flour
6 tablespoons cocoa (slightly heaping)
2 cups sugar
Pinch of salt
1/2 cup vegetable oil
2 cups sour milk, made by adding 2 tablespoons vinegar to milk
2 teaspoons baking soda
1 whole egg and 2 egg yolks

Preheat oven to 375 degrees.

Prepare sour milk as directed above, then add baking soda and let mixture stand.

Mix together all other ingredients, blending in a little of the milk before adding the eggs. Add rest of milk and stir until thoroughly blended. Batter will be thin.

Pour into two greased and floured 9-inch pans (or one 9 x 13 inch pan), and bake for approximately 30 minutes or until center of cake springs back when lightly touched.

Cool in pan 10 minutes; invert on cake rack. To freeze, wrap in plastic wrap and foil. Thaw unwrapped.

Serves 6 or more.

Faux Pots De Crème

Sinfully good, sinfully easy. There is absolutely no need to mention the marshmallows or the blender unless pressed!

1 cup miniature marshmallows
6-ounce bag semisweet chocolate bits
2 eggs
3/4 cup milk
3 tablespoons very strong coffee (try 2 teaspoons instant coffee and 1/4 cup hot water)
2 tablespoons rum or orange brandy

Place all ingredients except milk in container of blender. Scald milk (bring just to boiling point) and add to container. Blend on high for 2 minutes. Pour into six pots de crème or other small dessert dishes and chill overnight. Decorate with candied violets or orange zest if desired.

Serves 6.

Lime Tart

Serve this refreshing lime tart from a footed cake plate. Use a frozen deep dish pie shell or your favorite homemade pie crust.

1 frozen deep dish pie crust, thawed, or homemade pie dough
3 eggs
4 limes
2/3 cup sugar
2 tablespoons melted butter
1 cup whipping cream
3 tablespoons powdered sugar

Preheat oven to 400 degrees. Press thawed crust into 8- or 9-inch tart pan with removable bottom; bake until light gold, 10 to 15 minutes. Let cool. Lower oven temperature to 350 degrees.

Using a zester or a grater, remove zest only (not the bitter pith) from limes; place zest in medium mixing bowl. Slice the limes in half and juice on a reamer; remove any seeds and add juice to bowl. Add the eggs and sugar and whisk well until sugar is dissolved. Slowly add the melted butter and whisk until blended. Pour into the baked shell. Place tart pan on a cookie sheet and bake about 25-30 minutes, until custard begins to set. Remove from oven and cool. Cover and refrigerate or wrap well and freeze; thaw uncovered.

About two hours before dinner, whip the cream into soft peaks, gradually adding the powdered sugar. Cut the tart into 6 or 8 slices and serve with generous dollops of the sweetened cream.

Serves 6 or more.

Peach Pie

Homemade pie, just like Grandma used to make? Well, we've taken one shortcut for today's busy cook—frozen pie shells. If you have a favorite pie crust recipe, use it, of course. You'll need enough for a double crust.

2 deep-dish frozen pie shells, or homemade double crust
8 large ripe peaches
3/4 to 1 cup sugar, depending on sweetness of peaches, half granulated and
    half brown sugar
2 tablespoons cornstarch
1/2 teaspoon cinnamon, optional

Preheat oven to 400 degrees. Thaw pie shells.

To peel peaches easily, drop fruit in a big pot of boiling water for 1 minute, drain and rinse under cold water. Skins will slip off. Cut peaches in half, seed and slice each half into eighths. Place in large mixing bowl. Add cornstarch, sugar and optional cinnamon if desired. Mix gently.

Pile fruit into one of the pie shells. Carefully remove other pie shell from its pan and invert over the peaches. Pinch edges together and crimp with fork. Slice three steam slots in top pie crust and sprinkle with 1 teaspoon sugar. Place pie on a cookie sheet and bake 45 to 50 minutes, until crust is golden brown. Remove and let cool. Cover with plastic wrap and refrigerate overnight.

Cut pie into 6 or 8 slices and serve with best quality vanilla ice cream or whipped cream, if desired.

Serves 6 or more.

Cracker Crust Pecan Pie With Mocha Cream

Depending on your age, this is a variation of your mother's or grand mother's favorite dessert. You might like to flavor the topping with 1 tablespoon coffee liqueur; just eliminate the water, instant coffee and vanilla.

18 butter crackers, finely crushed
3 egg whites
1 cup sugar
1 teaspoon baking powder
1 cup coarsely chopped pecans
1 cup heavy cream
1 teaspoon water
2 teaspoons instant coffee
1 teaspoon vanilla
3 tablespoons powdered sugar

Beat egg whites until almost stiff. Gradually add sugar and beat until thick and glossy. Mix crackers, baking powder, pecans and vanilla. Fold into whipped egg whites with rubber spatula or wooden spoon. Spoon mixture into buttered 9-inch glass pie plate.

Bake in preheated 350-degree oven for 30 minutes. Remove and cool thoroughly on cake rack. Refrigerate up to 2 days.

Chill small bowl and beaters for whipping cream. Dissolve coffee in water, add vanilla. Put cream and coffee mixture or coffee liqueur into chilled bowl. Beat until cream mounds softly. Add powdered sugar, beat until stiff.

Spread on top of pie. Refrigerate several hours before serving.

Serves 6.

Pineapple-Coconut-Lemon Pie

These contrasting flavors and textures will please your guests. You might like to serve it after the earthy Italian Sausage, Shrimp and Rice Casserole.

1 unbaked 9-inch pie shell, your own or ready made
8-1/4 ounce can natural-juice pineapple cubes, drained
1/3 cup shredded coconut
1/3 cup light brown sugar
3 tablespoons melted butter
4-ounce box regular lemon pudding mix
1/2 cup sugar
1-1/2 cups water
2 eggs, separated
3 tablespoons lemon juice
2 teaspoons grated lemon peel
1 tablespoon butter
1/4 cup sugar
1/4 cup shredded coconut, toasted

Preheat oven to 425 degrees.

Lightly crush pineapple in small bowl, add coconut, brown sugar and butter; spread over bottom of pie shell. Bake for 15 minutes. Cool on cake rack.

In a small saucepan, blend pudding mix with 1/2 cup sugar. Lightly beat egg yolks and mix with water; stir into pudding mix and cook until thick. Remove from heat, add lemon juice, lemon peel and 1 tablespoon butter. Cool, stirring occasionally.

Beat egg whites until soft peaks form; gradually beat in remaining sugar until stiff peaks form. Fold egg whites into cooled filling; spoon into pie shell.

Chill several hours, preferably overnight. Sprinkle with toasted coconut before serving.

Serves 6.

Heavenly Hazelnut Cheesecake

Because this is a rich dessert, precede with simple first and second courses.

Crust
1-1/2 cups toasted hazelnuts (filberts)
12 square graham crackers, crushed
1/4 cup melted butter

Filling
4 egg whites
2/3 cup sugar
2 8-ounce packages cream cheese, softened
2 tablespoons Frangelico (hazelnut liqueur)

Topping
1-1/2 cups sour cream
2 tablespoons sugar
1 teaspoon flour
1 tablespoon Frangelico (hazelnut liqueur)
1 cup hazelnuts, coarsely chopped

Toast 1-1/2 cups hazelnuts in shallow pan in 425-degree oven for 10 minutes. Put nuts on small towel and roll up to rub nuts against each other to remove skins. Reduce oven temperature to 350 degrees.

Finely chop 1/2 cup nuts for crust. Coarsely chop remaining nuts and set aside for topping. Combine graham cracker crumbs, nuts and melted butter. Press crumbs onto bottom and about 1 inch up sides of buttered 8-inch springform pan. Beat egg whites until they start to mound. Gradually add sugar and beat until stiff and glossy. Beat in softened cream cheese and liqueur until smooth. Pour mixture into springform pan and bake in preheated 350-degree oven for 40 minutes.

Mix sour cream, sugar, flour and liqueur in small bowl. Carefully spoon on top of cheese filling after the 40-minute baking period; smooth top. Sprinkle with chopped hazelnuts. Return to oven for 30 minutes.

Cool cake thoroughly on cake rack. Cover with plastic wrap and store up to two days in refrigerator before serving. To freeze, wrap in plastic wrap and foil. Thaw in refrigerator after removing foil wrapping. Remove sides of pan and slide onto serving plate. Serve lightly chilled.

Serves 6.

Lucille's Shortbread

So simple, so delicious. Serve slender wedges of this buttery shortbread beside a dish of your favorite ice cream or sherbet topped with pureed fruit sauce.

1-1/4 cups unsifted flour
3 tablespoons cornstarch
1/4 cup sugar
1/2 cup butter

If using a food processor freeze butter before cutting into 8 pieces. Add flour, cornstarch and sugar to processor bowl and blend briefly with steel blade. Add pieces of frozen butter and process to a coarse crumb-like texture.

If not using a food processor, place flour, cornstarch, sugar and softened butter, cut into pieces, in a small bowl. With wet hands and a fork, work mixture into a coarse crumb-like texture.

Transfer crumb mixture to a 9-inch, removable-bottom pan or a 9-inch pie pan. Press firmly onto bottom and sides of pan. Press edge with a fork and prick bottom in numerous places. Bake in 325-degree oven for 40 minutes or until pale brown.

While still hot, cut into 12 wedges with a sharp knife. Sprinkle with 1 tablespoon sugar. Cool in pan, then store in airtight container at room temperature up to 1 week or freeze. Defrost uncovered.

Serves 6.

Dreamy Short Cookies

These melt-in-your-mouth crisp wafers are wonderful on a tray of assorted cookies and with any fresh fruit dessert.

1-1/4 cups flour
1/2 cup powdered sugar
1/2 cup cornstarch
1-1/4 sticks (10 tablespoons) butter, cut into 10 pieces
1/2 teaspoon vanilla
1/4 teaspoon salt
1/2 teaspoon cardamom, optional

Preheat oven to 300 degrees.

Put all ingredients into bowl and mix with electric mixer until smooth ball forms or use food processor fitted with steel blade.

Roll teaspoons of dough into balls and place on ungreased cookie sheets. Flatten with tines of fork dipped in flour.

Bake 20 minutes or until lightly browned on edges. Cool on cake rack. Store in an airtight container for several days or freeze.

Yields about 40 cookies.

Oatmeal Lace Cookies

This crisp cookie and the Dreamy Short Cookies complement each other and go well with any of our fruit desserts.

1/2 cup butter, softened
3/4 cup light brown sugar, packed
2 tablespoons flour
2 tablespoons milk
1/2 teaspoon almond extract
1-1/2 cups regular or quick oatmeal (not instant)

Preheat oven to 350 degrees.

In a small mixing bowl, cream together the butter and brown sugar. Add flour, milk and almond extract; mix well. Add oatmeal and mix briefly to incorporate.

Drop 6 teaspoons of dough, spaced far apart, on an ungreased cookie sheet. Bake 8 minutes. Refrigerate remaining dough.

Remove cookies from oven, let stand on sheet 1/2 minute. Flip cookies, one at a time, on sheet and roll quickly into a cylinder and place on a rack to cool. If the cookies on the sheet become too hard to roll, return to the oven for a few seconds to soften. Repeat baking and rolling with remaining dough.

Store in an airtight tin for several days or freeze in tin.

Yields about 24 cookies.

Cream Cheese And Apple Torte

This dessert seems to be just right whether you're serving an elegant or a simple meal. Choose an entree without a creamy sauce.

1/2 cup butter
1 cup sugar, divided
1 cup flour
1 teaspoon almond flavoring, divided
8 ounces cream cheese
1 egg
1/2 teaspoon cinnamon
4 cups thinly sliced apples (4 large Golden Delicious or Granny Smith)
1/3 cup sliced almonds

Cream butter, 1/3 cup sugar and 1/2 teaspoon almond extract. Blend in flour. Pat dough onto bottom and about 1 inch up the sides of an 8-inch springform pan.

Beat together cream cheese and 1/3 cup sugar. Add egg and 1/2 teaspoon almond extract; mix well and spread on pastry. Combine 1/3 cup sugar and cinnamon and toss with apples. Arrange apples on top of cream cheese and sprinkle with almonds.

Bake in preheated 450-degree oven for 10 minutes. Reduce heat to 400 degrees and bake for 25 minutes. Remove from oven to cake rack and run a sharp knife around rim. Cool to room temperature. Cover top with plastic wrap, then wrap with foil before storing up to 3 days in refrigerator or up to 3 weeks in freezer.

Remove foil from pan and bring to room temperature before serving.

Serves 6.

Homey Applesauce Cake

A real cake that evokes memories of childhood and seems to be the right ending for a "down-home" dinner.

1/3 cup butter
2/3 cup sugar
2 eggs, lightly beaten
1 cup applesauce
1 teaspoon vanilla
1-1/2 cups flour
1 tablespoon cocoa
1 teaspoon cinnamon
1/2 teaspoon ground cloves
1/4 teaspoon ground nutmeg
1/4 teaspoon salt

1/4 cup hot water
2 teaspoons baking soda
1/2 cup raisins
1/2 cup coarsely chopped walnuts

Icing
1/3 cup brown sugar
2 tablespoons cream or condensed milk
1 tablespoon butter
1/2 cup grated coconut
1/2 cup chopped walnuts

Preheat oven to 350 degrees. Grease and dust with cocoa a 9-inch glass baking dish. With electric mixer or food processor fitted with steel blade, cream together butter and sugar. Add eggs, applesauce and vanilla; mix just until blended.

Mix together flour, cocoa, cinnamon, cloves, nutmeg, salt, raisins and nuts. If using food processor, mix raisins and nuts with 1 teaspoon flour and add separately to batter before pouring into baking dish. Mix water and baking soda together. Add dry ingredients alternately with water and baking soda to the egg and applesauce mixture, blending well after each addition. Pour into prepared glass baking dish. Bake 45 minutes.

Ice cake while still warm. To make icing, mix brown sugar and cream in small saucepan, add butter and bring to a boil. Remove from heat and add coconut and nuts. Spread icing on cake and place under broiler until bubbly and lightly browned. (For a simpler topping, dust with powdered sugar before serving.) Cool on cake rack; wrap in plastic and foil and refrigerate or freeze.

Serves 6.

Pound Cake With Lemon Glaze

A tart-sweet treat. Serve as is or with fresh berries.

2 cups flour
2 teaspoons baking powder
1/2 teaspoon salt
1-1/2 cups sugar
1/2 cup butter (1 stick), softened
1/2 cup margarine (1 stick), softened
4 eggs
1/2 cup milk
1/2 teaspoon vanilla
1/2 teaspoon lemon extract

Lemon Glaze
1/2 cup sugar
2 tablespoons fresh lemon juice

Sift dry ingredients into large mixing bowl. Cut butter and margarine into pieces and add to bowl with remaining ingredients. Beat at medium speed for 10 minutes. Pour into well-greased and floured 9 x 5 x 3-inch loaf pan.

Bake in preheated 325-degree oven for 1 hour or until top of cake springs back when lightly touched. Cool on cake rack for 10 minutes.

Meanwhile, make Lemon Glaze: Mix sugar and lemon juice in small bowl; set aside.

Invert cake on cake rack and turn top-side up. With a toothpick or long, thin skewer make holes over top of cake; pour glaze over top. Cool cake completely, then wrap in plastic and refrigerate several days or wrap foil over plastic and freeze for several weeks.

To thaw, remove foil and bring to room temperature before serving.

Serves 6.

Index

Index

A

Almonds, 91, 108, 111, 158, 174
Anchovies, 28, 38, 39
Apple and Onion Casserole, 130
Apple Crisp, 15, 153
Apples, 57, 89, 114, 122, 129, 130, 143, 151, 152, 153, 174
Applesauce, 175
Apricots:
   canned, 72, 114, 150
   dried, 106
Artichoke hearts, 38, 108
Asparagus, 26, 55, 65, 133
Avocadoes, 33

B

Baby Burritos, 19, 49
Bacon, 59, 94, 99
Baked Brown Rice with Parsley, 18, 109
Backed Carrots Delicious, 128
Baked Fruit Compote, 150
Baked Sausages and Vegetables, 17, 80
Baked Spiced Corned Beef, 58, 95
Baked Sweet Carrots, 16, 127
Bananas, 89, 143
Barley, 73, 111
Barley and Mushroom Casserole, 111
Bean and Basil Salad, 34
Beans:
   black, 35
   green, 24, 79, 132, 134
   navy, 73
   red, 34

refried, 49
white, 34, 36, 81
Beef, 94, 95, 96, 97, 98
   corned, 95
   ground, 49, 93
Beef broth or stock, 59, 96, 99, 100, 109, 117
Beer, 99
Berries in Berry Sauce, 145
Biscuit mix, 153
Black Bean Tostados, 35, 74
Blender Hollandaise Sauce, 65
Blueberries, 143, 145, 151, 161
Bon Bon Chicken, 47
Bourekas, 17, **44**, 96
Brandy, 48, 100, 149
   orange, 165
   peach, 156
Bread crumbs, 69, 81, 85, 116, 125, 128, 130
   herbed, 124
Bread:
   French, 40
   Italian, 39, 135
   white, 162
Broccoli, 43, 55, 70, 132, 134
Bulgur wheat, 110
Bulgur Wheat with Chick Pea Pilaf, 17, **110**
Butter Crust Apple Kuchen, 18, 93, **152**
Butternut Squash and Carrot Mock Soufflé, 123

C

Cabbage, 68, 93
Cantaloupe, 76, 143, 147

Carrot and Apple Casserole, 129
Carrots, 27, 56, 58, 73, 79, 80, 81, 87, 93, 95, 123, 127, 128, 129
Casseri Toast, 40
Cassis, 150
Cauliflower, 132, 134
Celery, 56, 73, 75, 81, 87, 90, 93, 95, 98, 134
Ceviche, 17, **45**
Chardonnay, 146
Cheddar Cheese and Vegetable Soup, 18, **56**
Cheese and Pepper Crackers, 15, **42**
Cheese:
   bleu, 38
   Casseri, 40
   cheddar, 49, 56, 116, 119, 125
   cottage, 44, 83
   cream, 50, 124, 170, 174
   feta, 44
   Gruyere, 116
   Monterey Jack, 35, 43
   mozzarella, 31, 39, 70, 83, 144
   Parmesan, 25, 31, 70, 83, 87
   ricotta, 83
   Romano, 70
   string, 16, 38
   Swiss, 85
Cherries, 143
Cherry Tomatoes with Parsley Pesto, 25, 100
Chick Pea Salad, 17, 18, **27**, 96
Chick Peas (garbanzos), 27, 37, 70, 79, 110
Chicken, 47, 64, 65, 66, 67, 68, 69, 70, 72, 73, 74, 76, 77
   broth or stock, 52, 54, 55, 56, 57, 58, 70, 74, 77, 78, 79, 81, 86, 87,
   88, 89, 90, 91, 106, 107, 108, 109, 110, 111, 114, 116, 127
   livers, 48

Chicken and Cabbage, 16, **68**
Chicken and Smoked Sausage with Rice, 74
Chicken Breasts Bloch, 46, **69**
Chicken in Vinegar Sauce, 16, **67**
Chicken Lasagne, 70
Chicken Liver Pâté Devine, 18, **48**
Chili peppers, 45, 107
Chili powder, 77, 93, 98
Chili sauce, 49
Chinese hot oil, 47, 133
Chocolate Chocolate Cake, 163
Chocolate, semisweet, 159, 163, 165
Chutney, 89, 100
Ciambotto, 18, **29**, 72
Coconut, shredded, 169
Cod, 85
Cointreau, 156
Cold Cucumber and Yogurt Soup, 53
Cold Curried Tomato "Soup", 17, **51**
Cold Orange Soufflé, 16, **155**
Company Lamb Loaf with Yogurt-Dill Sauce, 18, **92**
Consommé, beef, 50
Cookies, Pepperidge Farm Lemon Crunch, 158
Corn, 43, 73, 93, 120, 133
Corn and Cheese Tart, 16, **43**
Corn Pudding, 15, **120**
Cous cous, 79
Cracker Crust Pecan Pie with Mocha Cream, 19, 100, **168**
Crackers:
  butter, 168
  graham, 170
Cranberries, 122

Cream Cheese and Apple Torte, 174
Cream:
   heavy or whipping, 55, 126, 152, 155, 156, 158, 168
   light, 58, 87, 159
   sour, 170
Cream of Asparagus or Broccoli Soup, 55
Cream of Carrot and Fresh Dill Soup, 16, 58
Creamed Bermuda Onions, 126
Crème Caramel with Fresh Fruit, 161
Crème de cassis, 143, 145, 156
Crostini, 16, 39
Crumb-Topped Baked Fish Fillets, 19, 85
Cucumbers, 33, 52, 53, 132, 133
Currants, 79, 89, 106, 162
Currant jelly, red, 100
Curried Cucumber Soup, 52
Custard Sauce, 16, 149, 151, 162

D

Deviled Eggs, 17, 26, 38
Devil's Food Cake Marie Larkin Connors, 164
Down-Under Golden Nugget Chicken, 72
Dreamy Short Cookies, 155, 172

E

Eggplant, 29, 30, 31, 131
Eggplant Parmesan, 31

F

Family Favorite Potatoes, 117
Faux Pots de Crème, 16, 165

Fennel, 80
Fettucine, 84
Figs, 91, 148
Figs Poached in Red Wine, 16, 79, **148**
Fish fillets, 45, 84, 85
Flounder, 45
Frangelico, 170
French Potato Salad, 17, **112**
Fresh Fruit Compote, 17, 91, **143**
Fresh Fruit Compendium, **140**
Frosted Consommé, 19, **50**, 69
Frozen Lemon Crunch Torte with Raspberry Sauce, 15, 69, 85, **158**
Fruited Lamb Curry, **89**

G

Garam masala, 107
Gertie's Eggplant Salad, 18, **30**
Gingered Melon, **147**
Grand Marnier, 149
Grapes, seedless green, 76
Grits, 119
Grits and Cheese Bake, **119**
Ground Beef Vegetable Garden Soup, **93**
Grouper, 45

H

Haddock, 85
Ham, 70, 78, 94
Harissa, 79
Hazelnuts, 170
Hearty Chicken Soup, 19, **73**

Heavenly Hazelnut Cheesecake, 170
Hollandaise sauce, 65
Homey Applesauce Cake, 19, **175**
Honeydew melon, 147
Horseradish, 46
Hot pepper sauce, 90
Hummous, 37

I

Ice cream:
   chocolate, 160
   coffee, 160
   vanilla, 145
Indian Rice, 15, **107**
Italian Sausage, Shrimp and Rice Casserole, 78
Italian Toast, 17, **135**

J

Jambalaya, 15, **77**

K

Kirsch, 143, 145, 161
Kiwi fruit, 143

L

Lamb, 89, 90, 91, 92
Lamb Shanks with Orzo, 90
Layered Mocha Ice Cream Pie, 160
Layered Vegetable Pâté, 33, 95
Lemon-Chocolate Charlotte, 46, **159**

Lemon pudding mix, 169
Lemony Bread Pudding, 16, **162**
Lentils, 93
Lime Tart, 18, **166**
Linguine, 47, 87, 98
Linguine and Meat Sauce Norwood, **98**
Liqueur, orange, 143
Low Calorie Lemon Mousse, 17, 96, **157**
Lucille's Shortbread, **171**

M

Macaroons, crushed Italian (amaretti), 147
Mangoes, 143
Mango chutney, 76
Marinated Asparagus with Deviled Eggs, 17, **26**
Marinated Green Bean and Zucchini Salad, 15, **24**, 78
Marinated Mixed Vegetables, 18, **134**
Marshmallows, miniature, 165
Melon, 38
Moroccan Lamb Stew, 15, **91**, 158
Mushrooms, 32, 70, 78, 87, 88, 98, 108, 111, 125
Mushrooms Au Gratin, **125**
Mystery Zucchini Soup, **59**

N

Nellie's Berry Cobbler, **154**
Noodles:
   lasagna, 70, 83
   egg, 118
Noodle Casserole, **118**
Nuts, salted, 38

O

Oatmeal, 173
Oatmeal Lace Cookies, 18, 76, **173**
Okra, 38, 77
Olives, cured, 16, 37, 38, 41, 125
Onion soup mix, dry, 72, 111
Onions, 24, 33, 41, 45, 49, 51, 52, 56, 57, 58, 73, 74, 75, 77, 78, 80, 82, 87
  96, 98, 126, 130
Orange juice, 122, 150
Orange marmalade, 100
Oranges, 95, 143
Oriental Beef Stew, 18, **97**
Orzo, 90
Ossobuco, 18, **86**, 158
Oven Parsley-Garlic Potatoes, **113**
Oysters, smoked, 38

P

Palm hearts, 132
Papaya, 143
Parsley, 25
Pasta and Veal Victoria, 18, **87**
Peach or Apple and Blueberry Crisp, 17, **151**
Peach Pie, 17, **167**
Peach preserves, 142
Peaches, 72, 146, 150, 151, 156, 167
Peaches in Spiced Chardonnay, **146**
Peachy Mustard Pears, 18, **142**
Peanut butter, 97
Peanuts, 97

Pears, 141, 142, 150
Peas, 73, 87, 88
Pecans, 160, 168
Pepperoni, 38
Peppers:
   hot, 83
   sweet (red, green or yellow), 27, 33, 41, 49, 56, 74, 77, 80, 82, 90, 93,
   98, 131, 132, 133, 134
Persian Rice, 18, **106**
Phyllo leaves, 44
Pie crust, frozen, 43, 166, 167
Pimento, 119
Pine nuts, 106
Pineapple, 89, 143, 169
Pineapple-Coconut-Lemon Pie, 18, **169**
Pistachios, 16
Pita wedges, 18
Plums, 150
Poached Pears with Raspberry Vinegar, 17, **141**
Polenta, **82**
Pork, 99, 100
Pork Carbonnade, 17, **99**
Potato and Fruit Gratin, 19, **95**
Potatoes, 80, 112, 113, 114, 115, 116, 117
Potatoes with Pizazz, **116**
Pound Cake with Lemon Glaze, 78, **176**
Prosciutto, 38
Prunes, 91

Q

Quick Berry Mousse with Peach Sauce, 18, **156**

Raisins, 175
  golden, 122
Raspberries, 145, 156, 158
Raspberry vinegar, 141, 144
Ratatouille, 131
Red snapper, 45
Rice:
  basmati, 107
  brown, 109
  long grain, 74, 77, 78, 93, 106, 107, 108
Rice Pilaf Deluxe, 108
Roast Chicken with Garlic and Lemon, 15, 31, **64**
Roast Pork with Game Sauce, 17, 33, **100**
Roast Potato Wedges with Herbs, 18, **115**
Roasted Peppers with Anchovies, 15, **28**
Round roast, 94
Rum, 165

S

Salmon, 46
Salmon Mousse with Mustard Mayonnaise, 46
Sardines, 38
Sausage, 68, 74, 77, 78, 79, 80, 81, 82, 94
Sausage and Cous Cous, 16, **79**
Sausage and Peppers, 82
Scallions, 106, 112, 133
Sea bass, 85
Seaside Fettucine, 84
Sesame paste, 47
Shallots, 112
Sherry, 111
Sherbet, lemon, 159

Shrimp, 38, 78, 84
Smothered Chicken with Garlic Linda, 66
Snow peas, 133
Spicy Apple Cake, 70
Spinach, 43, 83, 118, 124
Spinach Lasagne, 17, 83
Squash:
   butternut, 57, 122, 123
   hubbard, 57, 122
   yellow, 132, 134
Stifado, 17, 57, 96
Strawberries, 143, 144, 145, 156
Strawberries and Mozzarella, 16, 144
Stuffed Beef Roll, 18, 59, 94
Sue's Spinach Casserole, 124

T

Tahini, 37, 47
Tapas, 16, 38, 49
Tarragon Chicken Breast with Asparagus, 16, 65
Tarragon Chicken Salad with Fruit and Nuts, 16, 76
Tomatoes, 45, 51, 73, 74, 77, 81, 84, 93
   cherry, 25, 65, 132, 134
   Italian plum, 31, 33, 78, 79, 82, 83, 84, 90, 97, 98, 131
Tortellini, 41
Tortellini with Sesame Dressing, 41
Tostados, 35
Tuna, 75
Turkey, 75
Turkey Breast Tonnato, 75

V

Veal, 86, 87, 88
Veal Stew with Tiny Peas and Mushrooms, 88
Vegetables, pickled (giardinera), 38
Vegetables Vinaigrette, 15, 16, 97, **132**
Vermicelli, 110
Vermouth, 112

W

Walnuts, 25, 76, 110, 121, 133, 160, 175
White Bean Casserole, 81
White Bean Purée, 36
Winter Squash and Apple Soup, 17, **57**
Winter Squash with Fruit, 18, **122**
Won ton skins, 49

Y

Yogurt, 52, 53, 89, 92

Z

Zena's Pickled Mushrooms, 18, **32**
Zucchini, 24, 54, 59, 93, 121, 131, 132
Zucchini and Basil Soup, 54, 84
Zucchini and Walnut Sauté, 121

About the Authors

Nina Graybill and Maxine Rapoport are co-authors of *The Pasta Salad Book, Cold Soups,* and *Hearty Salads.* They live in Washington, D.C. For many years Ms. Rapoport has pursued a wide range of culinary interests, not the least of which is delighting family and friends with her gift for cooking. Ms. Graybill, a literary lawyer, cooks dinner and writes cookbooks whenever she finds the time.

For Additional Copies of

Cookbooks by Nina Graybill and Maxine Rapoport

Write: Farragut Publishing Company
2033 M Street N.W.
Washington, D.C. 20036

At $10.95 a copy plus shipping charge of $1.05 a copy, send me:

___ copy(ies) of *Enjoy! Make-Ahead Dinner Party Menus*
___ copy(ies) of *Hearty Salads*
___ copy(ies) of *Cold Soups*
___ copy(ies) of *The Pasta Salad Book*

Total ___ books; check enclosed for _____

Name_____

Address_____

City_____State_____Zip_____

Make check or money order payable to Farragut Publishing Company

- -

For Additional Copies of

Cookbooks by Nina Graybill and Maxine Rapoport

Write: Farragut Publishing Company
2033 M Street N.W.
Washington, D.C. 20036

At $10.95 a copy plus shipping charge of $1.05 a copy, send me:

___ copy(ies) of *Enjoy! Make-Ahead Dinner Party Menus*
___ copy(ies) of *Hearty Salads*
___ copy(ies) of *Cold Soups*
___ copy(ies) of *The Pasta Salad Book*

Total ___ books; check enclosed for _____

Name_____

Address_____

City_____State_____Zip_____

Make check or money order payable to Farragut Publishing Company